PHILIPPINES RETIREMENT

A COMPLETE BEGINNER'S GUIDE TO EXPATRIATE LIVING IN PARADISE

BY PHIL LIPINE

Philippines Retirement

Author: Phil Lipine
Publisher: Cineris Multifacet
Publication Date: 2024
ISBN: - 9798879265705

For inquiries and permissions, please contact:
Cineris Multifacet
cinerismultifacet@gmail.com

Design and Typesetting:
Cineris Multifacet

Cover Design:
Cineris Multifacet

Disclaimer:

Manufactured on Planet Earth.

First Edition: 2024

ISBN-13: - 9798879265705

19   54   95

Visit my website at
www.phillipine-investment.com
for more info on investing in the
Philippines!

TABLE OF CONTENTS

FOREWORD   **9**

x > My Background   11

xx > Why I Wrote This Book   15

INTRODUCTION   **19**

1 > Overview of Retiring in the Philippines   21

2 > Legal Scaffolding for Expatriates   25

PART I: PREPARING FOR THE MOVE   **29**

3 > Financial Planning for Retirement   31

4 > Cultural Acclimitazation   35

5 > Learning the Language   39

6 > Healthcare and Insurance   43

PART II: LEGALITIES AND LOGISTICS   **49**

7 > Visa and Residency Options   51

8 > Banking and Finance   55

9 > Property Laws and Restrictions   61

10 > Hiring Legal and Real Estate Professionals   65

PART III: BUYING AND BUILDING A HOME 71

11 > Choosing the Right Location   73

12 > Buying Property   77

13 > Designing Your Home 83

14 > Navigating Construction 87

15 > Utilities and Maintenance 91

PART IV: LIVING IN THE PHILIPPINES **97**

16 > Daily Life and Integration 99

17 > Expat Communities and Networking 103

18 > Travel and Adventure within the Philippines 107

19 > Safety and Security 111

PART V: FINANCIAL MANAGEMENT **117**

20 > Investment Opportunities 119

21 > Protecting Against Scams 123

22 > Estate Planning and Legal Affairs 127

PART VI: HEALTH AND WELL-BEING **131**

23 > Healthcare Services 133

24 > Wellness and Fitness 137

25 > Diet and Nutrition 141

**PART VII: CULTURAL AND SOCIAL INTE-
GRATION** **145**

26 > Engaging with the Local Community 147

27 > Religion and Spiritual Life 151

28 > Learning and Hobbies 155

PART VIII: LONG-TERM CONSIDERATIONS 159

29 > Renewal of Visas and Residency 161

30 > Planning for the Unexpected 165

31 > Reflections and Advice from Expatriates 169

CONCLUSION 173

32 > Embracing Your New Life 175

33 > A Thank You 179

APPENDICES 185

Appendix A: Checklist for Retiring in the Philippines 187

Appendix B: Useful Contacts and Resources 191

Appendix C: Glossary of Terms and Phrases 195

FOREWORD

x > My Background

From the moment I could understand the significance of a name, I felt an inexplicable pull towards a land whose name mirrored my own—Phil Lipine. It was as if my fate was encoded in those letters, a foreshadowing of an adventure that would define the very essence of my existence. My name, an accidental homage to the Philippines, became the illuminant that guided me to my second home, to a place that felt familiar before I had even set foot on its soil.

Growing up in a small American town, my dreams of the Philippines were fueled by stories of its emerald rice fields, bustling cities, and the warm, welcoming spirit of its people. I imagined the Philippines not just as a country, but as a promise of adventure and discovery. My name, Phil Lipine, was a constant reminder of this promise, a serendipitous connection to a distant land that beckoned me.

My adventure to the Philippines was not a mere act of travel; it was a pilgrimage to discover a part of myself that seemed to have always belonged there. When I finally made the voyage, stepping onto the Philippine soil for the first time, I felt an overwhelming sense of coming home. It was as though the land itself recognized me, welcoming me with open arms and a warmth that penetrated deep into my soul. Living in the Philippines has been an adventure of a lifetime. Beyond the breathtaking landscapes and the cultural richness, it was the people who truly made this country my home. Their resilience, joy, and unparalleled hospitality showed me the true heart of the Philippines. I learned to navigate the complexities of life here, embracing the challenges and celebrating the victories. From learning the nuances of Filipino culture to understanding the legalities of residency and property ownership, every step was a lesson that enriched my life immeasurably.

But my adventure is more than a personal tale of discovery and belonging. It is a narrative I feel compelled to share, to guide others who dream of a life in this beautiful archipelago. Through my story, I aim to illuminate the path for hard-working Americans who yearn for a retirement that promises more than just relaxation, but an extremely significant connection to a place that can offer them a new beginning. Writing this book is my way of paying forward the incredible gifts the Philippines has bestowed upon me. It is a step-by-step guide designed to navigate the complexities of retiring here, maximizing the value of your hard-earned money while avoiding the pitfalls that can ensnare unwary expatriates. From the legal complexities of visas and property ownership to the joys of integrating into the local community, this guide is a culmination of my experiences, lessons, and the wisdom of those who have walked this path before me.

My name, Phil Lipine, may have been a mere coincidence, but it charted the course of my life in ways I could never have imagined. It brought me to a land that has enriched my soul and given me a purpose beyond retirement—a purpose that I now share with you. This book is more than just a guide; it's an invitation to discover your own fate in the Philippines, to find a home in its islands, and to start to take in a life filled with adventure, warmth, and fulfillment.

As you turn these pages, I invite you to adventure with me—not just through the Philippines, but towards realizing your most ambitious dreams. Let this book be your compass, guiding you to a retirement that is not just a time of life, but a celebration of living to the fullest in a country that, perhaps, has been calling your name too.

xx > Why I Wrote This Book

Why I wrote this book is a question that goes to the heart of my adventure and the adventure I envision for countless hard-working Americans who have spent a life-time building a nest egg, dreaming of a retirement that goes beyond the ordinary. It's for those who see their golden years not just as a time to slow down, but as an opportunity to live fully, in a place that offers not just a lower cost of living but a richness of experience that can hardly be matched anywhere else on earth. This book is my labor of love, a detailed guide designed to help you realize the most ambitious of your retirement goals in the Philippines.

The dream of retiring in paradise is often marred by the complexities and challenges that come with moving to a new country. From navigating legal requirements and financial planning to integrating into a new culture and avoiding scams, the process can be daunting. My motivation to write this book stems from my own experiences and the realization that while the adventure is filled with potential pitfalls, each one can be navigated with the right knowledge and preparation.

My first encounter with the Philippines left me enamored with its natural beauty, warm people, and the incredible diversity of its landscapes and cultures. However, it was the stories of fellow expatriates that truly opened my eyes to the possibilities and challenges of retiring here. Some had seamlessly transitioned into their new life, while others faced hurdles they hadn't anticipated. These stories, both positive and negative, highlighted a common theme: the need for a comprehensive, step-by-step guide that could help future retirees maximize their retirement savings and avoid common mistakes. I wrote this book to fill that gap, to offer a roadmap that leads you through every stage of the process. From understanding the cost of living to selecting the right visa, from buying property to integrating into your local community, this guide is designed to help you make informed decisions that ensure your retirement savings go further while safeguarding you against scams and legal pitfalls that can be all too common for the unwary.

The Philippines offers an incredible opportunity for a fulfilling retirement, but like any country, it has its own set of rules, cultural nuances, and systems that can be complex. My aim is to demystify these, drawing on expert advice, legal insights, and personal anecdotes to provide a clear, actionable guide. Whether it's choosing where to live, understanding healthcare options, or planning your financial future here, this book covers it all, ensuring you're well-prepared for every aspect of your new life.

But beyond the practical advice, this book is also a confirmation of the spirit of adventure that defines the American dream. It's for those who've worked tirelessly, often putting aside their own desires for the sake of family and responsibility, and who now stand on the threshold of realizing their dreams. Retirement in the Philippines isn't just about stretching your dollars; it's about enriching your life with new experiences, friendships, and a deeper understanding of a culture that values respect, family, and community above all else.

This guide is more than just a how-to manual; it's a reflection of the possibilities that await when you dare to chase your dreams. It's a compilation of lessons learned, both my own and those of the many expatriates I've met along the way, shared with the hope that it will encourage and empower you to take the leap towards a retirement filled with adventure, peace, and fulfillment in the Philippines.

My adventure to writing this book was motivated by a desire to give back, to share the knowledge and insights I've gained so that others can avoid the pitfalls and start to take in the opportunities that the Philippines offers. It's my hope that through these pages, you'll find not just the practical advice you need but also the inspiration to pursue a retirement that's as rewarding as it is adventurous. Welcome to the adventure of a lifetime—your retirement in the Philippines.

INTRODUCTION

1 > Overview of Retiring in the Philippines

Creating a comprehensive adventure of retiring in the Philippines requires a deep dive into the country's allure as a retirement destination, its diverse climate, opulent culture, and the potential challenges expatriates might face.

Overview of Retiring in the Philippines

The Philippines, with its exhilarating archipelago of over 7,000 islands, offers an atlas of landscapes, cultures, and experiences that draw retirees from around the world. Its appeal as a retirement destination is multifaceted, encompassing the natural beauty, a warm tropical climate, the hospitality of its people, and the relatively low cost of living. However, like any country, it also presents its own set of challenges, from navigating the bureaucracy to understanding cultural nuances. Here's an overview.

The Appeal of the Philippines

Cost of Living: One of the primary attractions of retiring in the Philippines is the cost of living, which is significantly lower than in many Western countries. Housing, healthcare, and daily expenses allow retirees to enjoy a comfortable lifestyle without depleting their savings.

Natural Beauty and Climate: The Philippines is renowned for its stunning natural scenery, ranging from pristine beaches and coral reefs to mountainous terrain and tropical rainforests. The climate is tropical and generally warm and humid year-round, with a rainy season from June to November and a dry season from December to May. This allows for a variety of outdoor activities and a lifestyle close to nature.

Culture and Community: Filipino culture is a living blend of indigenous, Asian, and Spanish influences, known for its festivals, food, and arts. The sense of community and the Filipino hospitality is particularly strong, with expatriates often remarking on the warmth and welcoming nature of the local people. English is widely spoken, which eases communication and helps in adjusting to the new environment.

Potential Challenges

While the Philippines offers many advantages, prospective retirees should also consider the potential challenges they may face.

Healthcare: While urban areas like Manila and Cebu have modern healthcare facilities, access to healthcare in rural areas can be limited. Health insurance is a critical consideration, and expatriates may need to look at private health insurance options to ensure comprehensive coverage.

Infrastructure and Internet: Infrastructure quality can vary significantly across the country. While major cities are well-developed, some remote areas may lack reliable electricity, water supply, and internet connectivity, which could be a concern for those accustomed to the conveniences of developed nations.

Natural Disasters: The Philippines is prone to natural disasters, including typhoons, earthquakes, and volcanic eruptions. Understanding the risks and preparing for emergencies is essential for anyone considering moving to the country.

Bureaucracy and Legalities: Navigating the legal requirements for residency and property ownership can be complex. The Philippines has specific laws regarding foreign ownership of property, and the process of obtaining residency visas requires careful planning and understanding of the legal scaffolding.

Conclusion

Retiring in the Philippines offers a unique opportunity to enjoy a high quality of life in a beautiful setting, surrounded by a welcoming community. The affordability of living, coupled with the country's natural beauty and cultural richness, makes it an attractive destination for retirees seeking a peaceful and fulfilling retirement. However, it's important to approach the move with a thorough understanding of the potential challenges and to prepare accordingly. With proper planning and an open mind, retiring in the Philippines can be a rewarding and enriching experience.

2 > Legal Scaffolding for Expatriates

Writing an in-depth adventure of the legal scaffolding for expatriates retiring in the Philippines, especially focusing on visas, residency, and property ownership laws, requires a comprehensive understanding of Philippine immigration and real estate laws.

Legal Scaffolding for Expatriates in the Philippines

Visas and Residency

Special Resident Retiree's Visa (SRRV): The Philippines offers the Special Resident Retiree's Visa (SRRV), a program under the Philippine Retirement Authority (PRA), which allows foreign nationals to live in the Philippines indefinitely with multiple-entry privileges. There are several options under the SRRV, catering to different ages and financial capabilities:

- **SRRV Smile**: For active/healthy retirees, a deposit of USD 20,000 in a Philippine bank is required.
- **SRRV Classic**: For retirees who opt to use their deposit to purchase condominium units or long-term leases of house and lot, townhouses, etc. The required deposit varies from USD 50,000 to USD 10,000 depending on the retiree's age and the type of investment.

- **SRRV Human Touch**: For retirees needing medical care or services, a deposit of USD 10,000 is required, with proof of monthly pension.

Quota and Non-Quota Immigrant Visas: The Philippines also grants immigrant visas to foreign nationals under the quota system (limited slots annually) and non-quota system (for certain nationals and conditions, like marriage to a Filipino citizen).

Property Ownership Laws

Foreigners are restricted from owning land in the Philippines, but there are legal pathways to property ownership and investment:

- **Condominium Units**: Foreigners can own condominium units, provided that foreign ownership in a condominium project does not exceed 40%.
- **Long-term Lease**: Foreigners can lease land for up to 50 years, renewable once for an additional 25 years. This option is often utilized for residential purposes or agricultural investments.
- **Corporation or Partnership**: If a foreigner wants to invest in land, they can do so by forming a corporation with Filipino citizens, where the foreign equity does not exceed 40%.

Legal and Regulatory Considerations

- **Banking and Finance**: Expatriates should understand the banking system, including the process of opening bank accounts, transferring funds internationally, and managing taxes both in their home country and in the Philippines.
- **Healthcare**: Enrolling in a health insurance plan that provides adequate coverage in the Philippines is very important. The Philippine Health Insurance Corporation (PhilHealth) offers coverage for foreigners residing in the country, but many also opt for additional private health insurance.
- **Estate Planning**: Understanding Philippine laws regarding inheritance and estate planning is essential, especially since

foreign ownership laws affect how property and assets are managed and transferred.

Key Takeaways

- **Preparation and Research**: Before moving, it's very important to research and understand the legal requirements and options for visas, residency, and property ownership. Regulations can change, and having the most up-to-date information is necessary.
- **Professional Advice**: Consulting with legal professionals who specialize in immigration and real estate laws in the Philippines is strongly recommended. They can provide guidance tailored to an individual's circumstances, ensuring compliance with local laws and regulations.
- **Community Insights**: Engaging with expatriate communities already living in the Philippines can offer practical advice and insights into the process of settling in the country.

Conclusion

Retiring in the Philippines offers a unique and enriching experience for expatriates, but it requires careful planning and understanding of the legal scaffolding. The laws governing visas, residency, and property ownership are designed to protect both the interests of foreigners and the sovereignty of the Philippines. By navigating these legalities with thorough preparation and professional guidance, expatriates can enjoy a seamless transition to their new life in the Philippines.

PART I: PREPARING FOR THE MOVE

3 > Financial Planning for Retirement

Preparing for retirement, especially in a new country, requires careful financial planning and understanding of various factors including budgeting for the move, grasping the cost of living in the new location, and managing retirement funds efficiently.

Financial Planning for Retirement: Essentials of Financial Readiness

Budgeting for the Move

Initial Costs: Moving internationally involves several upfront costs, including visas, travel expenses, shipping for personal belongings, and initial accommodation expenses. It's very important to research and budget for these to avoid unexpected financial strain.

Emergency Fund: Before the move, ensure you have an emergency fund that covers at least 6-12 months of living expenses. This fund can help manage unexpected costs without dipping into your retirement savings.

Healthcare and Insurance: Factor in the costs of health insurance premiums and potential out-of-pocket medical expenses. Healthcare in the Philippines is generally affordable, but having comprehensive coverage is essential for peace of mind.

Understanding the Cost of Living

Housing: Whether you plan to rent or buy, housing costs can vary significantly depending on the location and type of accommodation. Research the costs in different areas of the Philippines to find a place that fits your budget and lifestyle needs.

Daily Living Expenses: Groceries, utilities, transportation, and entertainment should be included in your monthly budget. While the cost of living is relatively low in the Philippines, lifestyle choices can significantly affect your expenses.

Utilities and Communication: Electricity, water, internet, and mobile phone services are essential utilities to consider. Prices can vary, and it's wise to look into the average costs in your chosen area.

Retirement Funds Management

Income Sources: Identify your income sources in retirement, including pensions, social security benefits, investments, and any passive income streams. Understand how to access these funds in the Philippines, considering factors like international transfer fees and exchange rates.

Investments: Diversifying your investment portfolio can provide additional income and help protect against inflation. Consider consulting a financial advisor with experience in international retirement planning to make informed investment decisions.

Tax Implications: Understand the tax implications of retiring abroad, both in your home country and in the Philippines. This includes income tax, double taxation agreements, and any taxes on property or investments in the Philippines.

Currency and Inflation: Managing currency risk is very important, as fluctuations can affect your purchasing power. Inflation can also effect the cost of living, so factor this into your long-term financial planning.

Key Considerations

- **Comprehensive Budgeting**: Develop a detailed budget that includes all potential expenses and income sources. Regularly review and adjust your budget to reflect changes in your expenses or income.

- **Professional Advice**: Consult with financial advisors, tax professionals, and expatriate services to navigate the complexities of international retirement planning effectively.

- **Local Banking**: Consider opening a bank account in the Philippines for day-to-day expenses. Research banks that offer services for expatriates, including international transfers and currency exchange.

- **Legal and Financial Documentation**: Ensure all your financial and legal documents are in order, including wills, power of attorney, and healthcare directives, both in your home country and the Philippines.

Conclusion

Financial planning for retirement in the Philippines involves careful consideration of various factors, including budgeting for the move, understanding the cost of living, and effectively managing your retirement funds. By taking a proactive approach to financial readiness, you can ensure a comfortable and secure retirement in the Philippines. Planning, research, and professional advice are key to navigating the financial aspects of retiring abroad, allowing you to enjoy your retirement years with peace of mind.

This overview provides a foundational understanding of the financial planning needed for retiring in the Philippines, focusing on budgeting, cost of living, and retirement funds management. Detailed planning, ongoing management, and professional advice are essential to achieving financial readiness for a fulfilling retirement in the Philippines.

4 > Cultural Acclimitazation

Cultural acclimatization is a critical aspect of settling into a new country, especially for retirees seeking to make the Philippines their home. Understanding and embracing Filipino culture, traditions, and social norms can significantly ease the integration process, encouraging a sense of belonging and community.

Introduction to Filipino Culture

The Philippines is a country opulent in diversity, with a history shaped by indigenous, Spanish, American, and Asian influences. This blend has created a unique cultural mosaic that is evident in the country's traditions, language, celebrations, and daily life. At the heart of Filipino culture is "kapwa," a concept that focuses on shared identity and inner self, highlighting the importance of community and togetherness.

Core Values and Social Norms

Hospitality and Warmth: Filipinos are renowned for their hospitality and warmth, often going out of their way to make guests feel welcome. Visitors are treated with utmost respect and kindness, reflecting the value placed on "pakikisama" (harmony and smooth interpersonal relationships).

Respect for Elders: Respect for elders is deeply ingrained in Filipino society. Using "po" and "opo" when speaking to elders is a sign of respect, as is the "mano po" gesture, where one takes an elder's hand and brings it to their forehead as a form of greeting.

Family Orientation: The family is the cornerstone of social life, with extended families often living close to each other or in the same household. Family gatherings and celebrations are common, and taking care of elderly family members is a shared responsibility.

Festivals and Celebrations: The Philippines is famous for its living festivals, known as "fiestas," which celebrate patron saints, harvests, and historical events. These are marked by parades, dancing, music, and food, offering a fantastic way for expatriates to experience Filipino culture and community spirit.

Religion: The Philippines is predominantly Catholic, with religious observances playing a significant place in daily life. Attending Mass, celebrating religious holidays, and participating in religious festivals are integral parts of Filipino culture.

Language and Communication

While Filipino (based on Tagalog) and English are the official languages, the country is home to over 170 languages and dialects. Learning basic Filipino phrases can greatly aid in daily interactions and is appreciated by locals. Communication is often indirect, with great emphasis placed on not causing embarrassment or offense. Understanding non-verbal cues and the importance of saving face is very important for effective communication.

Food and Social Gatherings

Filipino cuisine is a reflection of the country's cultural diversity, with dishes that blend indigenous, Spanish, Chinese, and American influences. Sharing meals is a social event, and being invited to a Filipino home for a meal is a sign of friendship and trust. Participating in these gatherings, respecting dining etiquette, and showing appreciation for the food are important for cultural integration.

Navigating Challenges and Embracing Opportunities

Cultural Sensitivity: Being open to and respectful of cultural differences is key to acclimatization. It's essential to approach cultural norms and practices with curiosity and willingness to learn.

Community Engagement: Participating in community activities, volunteering, and joining local groups can help expatriates build connections and integrate more deeply into Filipino society.

Patience and Flexibility: Adjusting to a new culture takes time. Patience and flexibility are necessary as expatriates navigate the complexities of life in the Philippines, from bureaucratic processes to adapting to local customs.

Conclusion

Cultural acclimatization in the Philippines is an adventure of discovery, learning, and adaptation. By embracing the country's opulent traditions, values, and social norms, expatriates can find a sense of belonging in their new home. The warmth and hospitality of the Filipino people, combined with an openness to new experiences, pave the way for a fulfilling and integrated life in the Philippines. Through respect, understanding, and participation, expatriates can navigate cultural differences and enrich their retirement with the living culture and community spirit of the Philippines.

This overview touches on the essentials of cultural acclimatization for retirees in the Philippines, highlighting the importance of understanding and embracing local customs and traditions for a smooth transition and fulfilling life in their new home.

5 > Learning the Language

Learning the language in a new country is a key step towards successful integration, offering deeper connections with the community and a richer understanding of the culture. In the Philippines, with its opulent linguistic diversity and English as one of the official languages, the dynamics of language learning present both unique opportunities and challenges for expatriates. While a detailed exposition covering all aspects of Filipino and other regional languages, along with the importance of language for daily life and integration, would require extensive coverage, I will provide a structured overview to highlight the essentials of this adventure.

Introduction to the Linguistic Territory of the Philippines

The Philippines is a linguistically diverse country, home to over 170 languages and dialects. Filipino, which is based on Tagalog, acts as the national language and, along with English, is one of the two official languages of the country. English is widely used in government, education, and business, making it possible for English-speaking expatriates to navigate daily life relatively easily. However, learning Filipino or the relevant regional language can significantly enhance an expatriate's experience by facilitating deeper cultural immersion and interpersonal connections.

Basics of the Filipino Language

Filipino is an Austronesian language with a grammar structure that may be unfamiliar to speakers of Western languages. It is characterized by its use of verb-focus constructions, a feature that indicates the place of the actor, object, or direction in a sentence. Here are some foundational aspects:

- **Pronouns**: Filipino uses a set of personal pronouns that differ based on the level of formality and the inclusion or exclusion of the speaker and listener.
- **Verbs**: Verbs are inflected for aspect rather than tense, with focus on completed, ongoing, or intended actions.
- **Nouns**: Nouns do not have grammatical gender, simplifying the learning process for speakers of languages with gendered nouns.
- **Sentence Structure**: The basic sentence structure follows a verb-subject-object order, though this can vary depending on the focus of the sentence.

Learning basic phrases and expressions can help expatriates communicate in everyday situations, like shopping, dining, and socializing. Additionally, understanding common expressions of politeness and respect is very important in the Filipino context.

Regional Languages and Dialects

Beyond Filipino, the Philippines boasts a multitude of regional languages, with Cebuano, Ilokano, Hiligaynon, and Waray among the most widely spoken. Each region's language reflects its unique cultural heritage and identity. Expatriates living in areas where these languages are predominantly spoken may find it beneficial to learn some basics, as this gesture of respect can greatly facilitate community integration and appreciation of local traditions.

The Importance of Communication for Daily Life and Integration

Enhancing Social Interactions: Knowledge of the local language enables more meaningful interactions with Filipinos, who appreciate the effort to learn their language. It opens up opportunities for genuine conversations, deeper friendships, and a better understanding of the local mindset and way of life.

Navigating Daily Life: While English may suffice for most transactions and interactions, speaking the local language can be especially helpful in rural areas or for dealing with bureaucracy, where English proficiency may be limited.

Cultural Immersion: Language is a gateway to culture. Learning Filipino or a regional language allows expatriates to appreciate nuances in humor, poetry, music, and traditions that are lost in translation, enriching their cultural experience.

Tips for Language Learning

- **Start with the Basics**: Focus on practical vocabulary and phrases that can be used in daily conversations. Language apps, online courses, and textbooks can provide a good foundation.
- **Practice with Locals**: Engage in language exchange or conversation practice with Filipino friends and neighbors. This real-world practice is invaluable for developing fluency and confidence.
- **Immerse Yourself**: Watch Filipino TV shows, listen to local music, and read in the language to enhance your listening and comprehension skills.
- **Be Patient and Persistent**: Language learning is a gradual process. Celebrate small victories and remain committed to continuous improvement.

Conclusion

Learning Filipino or the relevant regional language as an expatriate in the Philippines is more than just acquiring a new skill; it's a step towards deeper integration, richer cultural experiences, and building stronger connections within the community. While English may act as a comfortable lingua franca, the effort to speak the local language is a powerful gesture of respect and openness that can transform an expatriate's experience in the Philippines. By embracing the linguistic diversity of their new home, expatriates can navigate daily life with greater ease and immerse themselves fully in the living cultural atlas of the Philippines.

6 > Healthcare and Insurance

Navigating the healthcare system and understanding insurance options are very important aspects of preparing for health needs abroad, especially for expatriates planning to retire in the Philippines. The Philippine healthcare system offers both public and private options, with varying levels of accessibility, quality, and cost.

Understanding the Philippine Healthcare System

The healthcare system in the Philippines is a mixed public-private system. The public healthcare system is managed by the Department of Health (DOH) and provides services through a network of public hospitals and rural health units. The Philippine Health Insurance Corporation (PhilHealth), a government-owned and controlled corporation, is the primary provider of health insurance in the country, offering coverage for a range of outpatient and inpatient services. However, the coverage can be limited, and many opt for additional private insurance.

Private healthcare in the Philippines is known for its higher quality of care, with private hospitals and clinics offering modern facilities and shorter waiting times. Many healthcare professionals in the Philippines are fluent in English, easing communication barriers for expatriate retirees.

Health Insurance Options for Expatriates

PhilHealth: Expatriates residing in the Philippines can register with PhilHealth to avail of basic health insurance coverage. PhilHealth coverage includes a portion of hospitalization costs, certain outpatient services, and surgeries, but it often does not cover the full cost of treatment, especially in private hospitals.

Private Health Insurance: Many expatriates choose to supplement PhilHealth coverage with private health insurance, which can offer more comprehensive coverage, including access to private hospitals, broader services, and higher claim limits. International health insurance plans designed for expatriates can provide extensive coverage, including medical evacuation and repatriation, which might be important for those living in more remote areas of the Philippines.

Travel Insurance: Short-term visitors or those in the process of transitioning to long-term residency might consider travel insurance with medical coverage. However, it's important to transition to a more permanent health insurance solution for long-term stays.

Preparing for Health Needs Abroad

Understanding Your Health Insurance Coverage: Thoroughly research and understand the terms of your health insurance, including coverage limits, exclusions, and the process for filing claims. Consider the need for supplemental policies to cover any gaps.

Choosing Healthcare Providers: Research hospitals and clinics, especially those within your insurance network, to find reputable healthcare providers. Private hospitals in major cities like Manila, Cebu, and Davao are known for their high standards of care.

Managing Prescription Medications: If you rely on prescription medications, research their availability in the Philippines. Some medications might have different brand names or might not be as readily available. Discuss with your healthcare provider about obtaining a sufficient supply or finding local equivalents.

Emergency Preparedness: Know the contact details of your nearest hospital or clinic, and understand the procedure for emergencies, including ambulance services and emergency hotlines. Consider a medical alert system if you have a chronic condition that might require immediate attention.

Regular Health Check-ups: Once settled, regular check-ups with healthcare providers are important for maintaining health and catching any potential issues early. This is also a good opportunity to build a relationship with local healthcare professionals.

Key Considerations

- **Cost of Healthcare**: While healthcare in the Philippines is generally more affordable than in many Western countries, costs can vary widely between public and private care. Ensure that your health insurance plan adequately covers potential healthcare costs.

- **Quality of Care**: The quality of healthcare can vary significantly across different regions of the Philippines. Urban areas tend to have better facilities and more specialists compared to rural areas.

- **Cultural and Language Barriers**: While English is widely spoken in the healthcare sector, there may still be cultural differences in medical practices and patient care. Being open and communicative with your healthcare providers can help bridge any gaps.

Conclusion

For expatriates retiring in the Philippines, navigating the healthcare system and securing adequate health insurance are essential steps in ensuring a safe and healthy life abroad. By understanding the available healthcare services, insurance options, and preparing for health needs, retirees can enjoy their time in the Philippines with peace of mind. Planning, research, and consultation with professionals are key to successfully managing healthcare needs in a new country.

PART II: LEGALITIES AND LOGISTICS

7 > Visa and Residency Options

Navigating the visa and residency options in the Philippines involves understanding a variety of visa types, each with its own set of requirements and application processes. This complex territory is designed to accommodate different needs, from short-term visits to long-term residency.

Tourist Visa

Overview: The Tourist Visa is typically issued for those who wish to stay in the Philippines for a short period, usually for tourism, business, or visiting relatives.

Requirements:
- Passport valid for at least six months beyond the intended stay.
- Return ticket to the home country or onward destination.
- Evidence of financial capacity to support the stay in the Philippines.

Application Process: Application for a tourist visa can be made at Philippine embassies or consulates abroad. The process involves submitting the required documents, paying the visa fee, and attending an interview if necessary.

Special Resident Retiree's Visa (SRRV)

Overview: The SRRV is designed for foreign nationals who wish to retire in the Philippines and offers a path to permanent residency. There are different categories under the SRRV, catering to retirees of varying ages and financial capacities.

Requirements:
- **SRRV Smile**: For active retirees, a deposit of USD 20,000 in a Philippine bank.
- **SRRV Classic**: Requires a deposit of USD 10,000 to USD 50,000, depending on age and pension status, which can be used towards the purchase of a condominium unit or long-term lease of a property.
- **SRRV Human Touch**: For retirees needing medical care, a deposit of USD 10,000 and proof of a monthly pension of at least USD 1,500.
- **SRRV Courtesy**: For former Filipino citizens and foreign nationals aged 50 years or older who have served in foreign diplomatic corps, a deposit of USD 1,500.

Application Process: The application is processed by the Philippine Retirement Authority (PRA). Applicants must submit the required documents, including a valid passport, proof of the required deposit, medical clearance, and police clearance from their country of origin.

9(g) Pre-arranged Employment Visa

Overview: This visa is for foreign nationals who are coming to the Philippines to engage in lawful employment, with a Philippine company acting as the petitioner.

Requirements:
- Employment contract or offer approved by the Department of Labor and Employment (DOLE).
- Passport valid for at least six months beyond the intended stay.
- Various corporate documents from the petitioner company.

Application Process: The application involves coordination between the employer and the Bureau of Immigration. The employer must file a petition on behalf of the applicant, accompanied by the required documents.

13(a) Non-Quota Immigrant Visa

Overview: The 13(a) Visa is for foreign nationals married to Filipino citizens, allowing them to reside permanently in the Philippines.

Requirements:
- Marriage certificate authenticated by the Philippine Statistics Authority (PSA) or the Philippine embassy if married abroad.
- Passport valid for at least six months beyond the intended stay.
- Medical examination and police clearance.

Application Process: The application is submitted to the Bureau of Immigration in the Philippines or a Philippine embassy or consulate abroad. It involves an interview and submission of the necessary documents.

Quota Immigrant Visa

Overview: The Quota Immigrant Visa is granted to nationals of countries with which the Philippines has diplomatic relations, with a yearly limit of 50 visas per nationality.

Requirements:
- Proof of financial capacity and investment in the Philippines.
- No record of criminal activity and good health.
- Passport valid for at least six months beyond the intended stay.

Application Process: Applicants must file their application with the Bureau of Immigration, providing the necessary documentation to prove their eligibility under this category.

Permanent Resident Visa

Overview: Permanent residency can also be obtained through other specific visas, like the 13(g) visa for former Filipino citizens and their dependents.

Requirements and Application Process: Varies based on the specific visa category, generally requiring proof of eligibility, financial capacity, health clearance, and a valid passport.

Key Considerations

- **Timelines and Processing**: Visa and residency application processes can be time-consuming, requiring patience and attention to detail.
- **Legal and Professional Advice**: Consulting with immigration lawyers or professionals can provide valuable assistance and ensure compliance with all requirements.
- **Updates and Changes**: Immigration policies and requirements can change; staying informed through official channels is very important.

Conclusion

The Philippines offers a variety of visa and residency options tailored to meet the needs of tourists, retirees, workers, and those seeking permanent residency through marriage or investment. Understanding the specific requirements and application processes of each visa type is essential for a smooth transition to life in the Philippines. Proper preparation, adherence to legal requirements, and possibly the assistance of professionals can help navigate this complex process successfully.

8 > Banking and Finance

Navigating banking, finances, and tax obligations is a critical aspect of relocating to a new country, particularly for expatriates planning to move to the Philippines. Understanding how to efficiently manage these financial necessities can significantly ease the transition and ensure a smooth settlement process. While an exhaustive adventure would require detailed research beyond the scope of this platform, I will provide a comprehensive overview of setting up banking, transferring funds internationally, and managing taxes for expatriates in the Philippines.

Setting Up Banking in the Philippines

Choosing a Bank: The Philippines hosts a range of banking institutions, from local banks with extensive national networks like BDO Unibank and Bank of the Philippine Islands (BPI), to international banks with local branches like Citibank and HSBC. Expatriates should consider factors like the availability of English-speaking staff, online banking facilities, branch and ATM accessibility, and the range of financial services offered when choosing a bank.

Opening a Bank Account: To open a bank account in the Philippines, expatriates typically need to present:
- A valid passport.
- A Philippine visa indicating residency status.
- Proof of address in the Philippines (e.g., utility bill, lease agreement).

- Alien Certificate of Registration Identity Card (ACR I-Card) for foreign residents.
- Initial deposit amount, which varies by bank and account type.

Some banks may have additional requirements, so it's advisable to check directly with the bank for their specific account opening criteria.

Transferring Funds Internationally

Remittance Services: The Philippines is one of the world's largest markets for remittance flows. Consequently, numerous services facilitate international money transfers, including banks, online platforms like PayPal, TransferWise (now Wise), and remittance centers like Western Union and MoneyGram. These services vary in terms of fees, exchange rates, and delivery times.

Bank Transfers: For larger transactions, like property purchases or significant investments, bank-to-bank transfers are commonly used. SWIFT transfers are a secure method for international money transfers, although fees and exchange rate margins should be taken into consideration.

Online Money Transfer Services: Digital platforms offer competitive fees and exchange rates compared to traditional banks. They are particularly useful for regular, smaller transfers, like sending money for daily expenses or family support.

Managing Taxes

Philippine Tax Residency: Understanding tax residency is very important for expatriates. Generally, individuals are taken into consideration Philippine tax residents if they stay in the country for more than 180 days in a calendar year, subjecting them to tax on their worldwide income. Non-residents are taxed only on their Philippine-sourced income.

Income Tax: The Philippines has a progressive income tax system for residents, with rates ranging from 0% to 35% as of the last update. Expatriates working in the Philippines should obtain a Tax Identification Number (TIN) and file annual income tax returns.

Double Taxation Agreements (DTAs): The Philippines has DTAs with many countries, which can prevent double taxation of income. Expatriates should consult with a tax professional to navigate these agreements and understand how they affect their tax liabilities.

Estate and Inheritance Taxes: Understanding the implications of estate and inheritance taxes in the Philippines is important for long-term financial planning. The country imposes an estate tax on the transfer of the deceased's estate to their heirs, with certain exemptions and rates that have been subject to change.

Financial Planning and Investment

Savings and Investments: Beyond basic banking, expatriates should consider their broader financial planning and investment strategies. The Philippines offers investment opportunities in real estate, stocks, mutual funds, and other financial instruments. Seeking advice from a financial advisor familiar with both Philippine and home country regulations is advisable.

Insurance: Exploring insurance options, including health, property, and life insurance, is an essential part of financial planning in the Philippines. Insurance can provide an additional layer of security for expatriates and their families.

Key Considerations

- **Currency Fluctuations**: Expatriates should be mindful of currency exchange rates and their effect on transfers and investments.
- **Regulatory Compliance**: Staying informed about changes in banking regulations, tax laws, and financial compliance requirements is very important for expatriates living in the Philippines.

- **Professional Advice**: Consulting with financial advisors, tax professionals, and legal experts can provide valuable insights and help navigate the complexities of managing finances and taxes in an international context.

Conclusion

Successfully managing banking, finances, and taxes is foundational to a smooth and secure expatriate experience in the Philippines. By carefully selecting banking services, understanding the best practices for international fund transfers, and complying with tax obligations, expatriates can protect their financial interests and enjoy their new life in the Philippines. Comprehensive planning, ongoing education, and professional advice are key to navigating the financial territory effectively.

9 > Property Laws and Restrictions

Navigating property laws and understanding the restrictions on foreign ownership in the Philippines are very important for expatriates interested in acquiring property in the country. The Philippines offers a living real estate market with opportunities for investment and residence, but it also imposes specific limitations on foreign ownership designed to protect national interests. This guide aims to elucidate these restrictions and outline legal pathways for foreigners to acquire property, ensuring compliance with Philippine laws.

Overview of Property Ownership Restrictions for Foreigners

The Philippine Constitution and the Republic Act No. 7042, or the Foreign Investments Act of 1991, as amended, set forth the legal scaffolding governing property ownership by foreigners. Key restrictions include:

- **Land Ownership**: Foreign nationals and foreign corporations are generally prohibited from owning land in the Philippines. This restriction is grounded in the desire to ensure land remains in the hands of Filipino citizens. However, there are exceptions and legal pathways for foreigners to indirectly own land or enjoy its use.

- **Ownership of Condominium Units and Townhouses**: While direct land ownership is restricted, foreigners are allowed to own condominium units or townhouses within buildings or projects, provided that foreign ownership in a condominium project does not exceed 40% of the total project.

- **Long-Term Leases**: As stated in a previous section, foreigners can lease land in the Philippines for residential purposes. The lease can be up to 50 years, renewable once for an additional 25 years. This arrangement is often used by foreigners who wish to build a house or use land for agricultural, business, or tourism purposes.

Legal Pathways to Property Acquisition

Acquisition of Condominium Units: Purchasing a condominium unit is the most straightforward method for a foreigner to invest in Philippine real estate. The process involves selecting a unit, making the necessary financial arrangements, and completing the sale documentation through a deed of absolute sale.

Long-Term Land Leases: Entering into a long-term lease agreement with a Filipino landowner allows foreigners to use land for an extended period. This requires drafting a lease agreement that specifies the terms, conditions, and duration of the lease, subject to legal limitations.

Incorporation of a Philippine Corporation: Foreigners can indirectly own land through the incorporation of a Philippine corporation. By law, such a corporation can be up to 40% foreign-owned, with the remaining 60% owned by Filipino citizens. The corporation can then legally purchase and own land in the Philippines.

Acquisition Through Inheritance: Foreigners married to Filipino citizens can inherit land as legal heirs, subject to the Philippine laws on inheritance and succession.

Process of Property Acquisition

1. **Due Diligence**: Before purchasing property, conduct thorough due diligence to verify the title, check for any encumbrances, and ensure compliance with zoning and land use regulations.

2. **Financing and Payment**: Understand the financing options available, including bank financing in the Philippines. Foreigners typically need to provide a significant down payment.

3. **Sale Documentation**: The sale is formalized through a Deed of Absolute Sale, which should be notarized and registered with the local Registry of Deeds. Transfer taxes, registration fees, and other charges must be settled to complete the transaction.

4. **Title Transfer**: Once the sale is registered, the Land Registration Authority issues a new title in the name of the buyer.

Key Considerations

- **Legal and Professional Advice**: Engage the services of a reputable real estate lawyer to navigate the complexities of property acquisition, ensuring that all legal requirements are met.

- **Understanding Restrictions**: Familiarize yourself with local regulations and restrictions, including those related to land use, environmental protection, and development standards.

- **Tax Implications**: Be aware of the tax implications of property ownership, including real property taxes, capital gains tax, and documentary stamp taxes.

Conclusion

While foreign ownership of property in the Philippines comes with restrictions, there are legal pathways and options available for expatriates to invest in or use Philippine real estate. Understanding these laws and regulations is paramount to ensuring a lawful and secure property acquisition process. With careful planning, due diligence, and professional guidance, foreigners can navigate the legal territory to find a suitable property solution that meets their needs and complies with Philippine law.

10 > Hiring Legal and Real Estate Professionals

Introduction

Relocating to the Philippines or investing in its real estate market demands navigating a complex legal territory, especially for foreigners unfamiliar with the local laws and regulations. Legal and real estate professionals hold a very important place in ensuring that your investments are secure and your residency is established without legal hitches. This guide outlines how to find and choose the right support for legal and property matters in the Philippines.

Understanding the Need for Professional Support

Legal Professionals: Legal advisors or lawyers are indispensable in understanding the nuances of Philippine law concerning visas, residency, property acquisition, taxation, and estate planning. They ensure compliance with local regulations, help in drafting and reviewing contracts, and provide representation in legal matters.

Real Estate Professionals: Real estate agents and brokers provide valuable insights into the property market, assist in finding properties that meet your criteria, and guide you through the buying or leasing process. They can also offer advice on market trends, pricing, and negotiation strategies.

Finding Legal and Real Estate Professionals

Referrals and Recommendations: Start by asking for referrals from expatriates who have successfully navigated the process, as well as from local contacts and business associations. Personal recommendations can provide reliable leads to competent professionals.

Professional Directories and Associations: Use directories from professional associations like the Integrated Bar of the Philippines (IBP) for lawyers and the Philippine Association of Real Estate Boards (PAREB) for real estate professionals. These organizations often list certified members with their specialties and contact information.

Online Research and Reviews: Websites, forums, and social media groups focused on expatriate living in the Philippines can be opulent sources of information and reviews about legal and real estate professionals.

Embassies and Consular Offices: Some embassies and consular offices offer lists of local attorneys and real estate professionals who speak your language and are familiar with assisting expatriates.

Choosing the Right Professional

Credentials and Experience: Verify the professional's credentials, ensuring they are licensed and in good standing with their respective professional associations. Look for individuals with experience in dealing with expatriates and familiarity with the specific legal or real estate issues you face.

Specialization: Given the complexity of laws and real estate transactions, professionals specializing in the area of your need—be it immigration law, property law, or specific types of real estate—can offer more nuanced advice and services.

Communication Skills: Choose professionals who communicate clearly and effectively in your language, ensuring that you fully understand the legal and transactional details.

Reputation and Track Record: Assess the professional's reputation in the industry through reviews, testimonials, and, if possible, direct feedback from previous clients. A track record of success and ethical practice is very important.

Fee Structure: Understand how the professional charges for their services—whether it's a flat fee, hourly rate, or commission. Ensure transparency and agreement on fees to avoid surprises.

Engaging Legal and Real Estate Professionals

Initial Consultation: An initial meeting or consultation, often offered for free or at a nominal charge, can help you assess the professional's expertise and compatibility with your needs.

Clear Communication of Needs: Be clear about your objectives, expectations, and any concerns you have. A good professional should be attentive to your needs and provide clear, actionable advice.

Agreement and Representation: Before formally engaging their services, ensure you have a written agreement outlining the scope of services, fees, and any other important terms of engagement.

Ongoing Communication: Maintain open lines of communication with your legal and real estate professionals throughout your dealings. Regular updates and prompt responses to queries are signs of good service.

Conclusion

Finding and choosing the right legal and real estate professionals in the Philippines is a critical step in ensuring the success of your property investments and legal compliance. By following a systematic approach to identifying, evaluating, and engaging these professionals, expatriates can navigate the complexities of legal and real estate transactions with confidence. Remember, the right professional support not just offers peace of mind but also safeguards your interests in a new country.

PART III: BUYING AND BUILDING A HOME

11 > Choosing the Right Location

       Choosing the right location for retirement in the Philippines requires careful consideration of various factors that can effect your quality of life. The country offers a diverse array of locations, from bustling cities to tranquil beachfronts and rural highlands, each with its unique appeal and challenges.

Climate

The Philippines is characterized by a tropical climate with three main seasons: the hot dry season (March to May), the rainy season (June to November), and the cool dry season (December to February). The country's geography also results in regional climate variations.

- **Temperature and Humidity**: Consider whether you prefer the warmer coastal areas or the cooler, less humid climates found in higher elevations like Baguio or Tagaytay.
- **Rainfall and Typhoon Risk**: Some areas are more prone to heavy rainfall and typhoons. Understanding the regional differences in weather patterns is very important, especially if you wish to avoid the extremes of the tropical climate.

Amenities and Accessibility

The availability of amenities and the ease of access to essential services can greatly influence your living experience.

- **Healthcare Facilities**: Proximity to reputable healthcare facilities is a must, especially for those with ongoing medical needs. Urban areas typically offer better healthcare services than rural regions.
- **Shopping and Dining**: Access to shopping centers, grocery stores, and restaurants can add convenience and enjoyment to your retirement lifestyle. Larger cities and tourist areas often provide a wider range of options.
- **Transportation**: Consider the availability of public transportation, especially if you do not plan to drive. Some areas may also offer better connectivity to international airports, facilitating travel back to your home country or exploring other parts of Southeast Asia.

Cost of Living

The cost of living can vary significantly across different parts of the Philippines. Urban areas like Metro Manila tend to be more expensive than rural locations. Assessing your budget against the cost of living in a prospective area is essential to ensure a comfortable retirement.

- **Housing Costs**: Whether renting or buying, housing costs will be a major component of your monthly expenses. Research the property market in your areas of interest to find the best value.
- **Daily Expenses**: Utilities, groceries, transportation, and entertainment can vary in cost. Smaller cities and rural areas may offer a lower cost of living, providing more bang for your buck.

Safety and Security

While the Philippines is generally a safe country for expatriates, safety concerns can vary by region. It's important to research and consider the safety of potential retirement locations.

- **Crime Rates**: Urban areas may have higher crime rates, but this can vary widely. Online forums, expatriate groups, and local news outlets can provide insights into the safety of different areas.

- **Natural Disasters**: The Philippines is prone to natural disasters like typhoons, earthquakes, and volcanic eruptions. Understanding the geographical risks and the local community's preparedness is very important.

Community and Social Integration

For many retirees, the ability to integrate into the local community and find social support is necessary to their happiness.

- **Expat Community**: Some areas are popular among expatriates and may offer a more immediate sense of community. Cities like Cebu, Davao, and parts of Luzon have established expat populations.
- **Local Culture and Language**: Consider your desire and ability to immerse yourself in the local culture and learn the language. Areas with a significant expatriate presence may offer more English-speaking locals and services tailored to foreign residents.

Leisure and Recreation

Your interests and hobbies should also hold a part in your decision. The Philippines offers a wide range of recreational activities, from diving and beach activities to golfing, hiking, and cultural adventure.

- **Natural Attractions**: Proximity to beaches, mountains, and natural parks can offer daily enjoyment and opportunities for physical activity.
- **Cultural and Historical Sites**: For those interested in the opulent cultural heritage of the Philippines, cities with historical sites, museums, and cultural events may be more appealing.

Conclusion

Selecting the right location for retirement in the Philippines is a deeply personal decision that requires balancing various factors, including climate, amenities, cost of living, safety, community integration, and leisure opportunities. Thorough research, coupled with visits to potential retirement spots, can help you make an informed choice that aligns with your lifestyle preferences and retirement goals. Remember, the perfect retirement location is one that meets your unique needs and ensures a fulfilling and joyful retirement experience.

12 > Buying Property

Buying property, especially in a foreign country like the Philippines, involves a series of structured steps, each very important to ensure a smooth and legally sound transaction. A comprehensive guide covering this process can empower potential buyers to navigate the complexities of the real estate market confidently.

Step 1: Define Your Criteria

Begin by clearly defining what you're looking for in a property, including type (e.g., condominium, house, land), location, size, amenities, and budget. Consider factors like proximity to healthcare, accessibility, community, and potential for appreciation.

Step 2: Research and Due Diligence

Market Research: Familiarize yourself with the real estate market in your chosen location. Look into average prices, market trends, and future development plans that could affect property values.

Legal Restrictions: Understand the legal restrictions on foreign property ownership in the Philippines, particularly regarding land ownership. Foreigners can own condominium units, provided foreign ownership within the condominium corporation does not exceed 40%.

Step 3: Find a Reputable Real Estate Agent

A knowledgeable local real estate agent can be invaluable, especially for foreigners. Look for agents with experience working with expatriates, a strong track record, and knowledge of the local market and legal requirements.

Step 4: Property Search

With the help of your agent, start searching for properties that match your criteria. Online real estate platforms, listings, and your agent's network can provide various options. Visit properties to get a feel for the location, neighborhood, and the property itself.

Step 5: Legal and Professional Assistance

Engage a real estate lawyer to help navigate the legal aspects of the purchase. They can conduct due diligence on the property, verify titles, check for encumbrances or legal issues, and ensure the transaction complies with local laws.

Step 6: Make an Offer

Once you've identified a property that meets your criteria, make an offer through your agent. Be prepared to negotiate the price and terms of the sale. Once the seller accepts your offer, a Reservation Agreement is often signed, and a reservation fee is paid to hold the property.

Step 7: Due Diligence

Your lawyer and agent will conduct thorough due diligence, including verifying the property's legal status, ensuring the title is clean and free of liens, and checking zoning regulations and any association dues or restrictions.

Step 8: Sales Agreement

After due diligence confirms the property's eligibility for sale, you'll move to draft and sign the Sales Agreement or Contract to Sell. This document outlines the terms of the sale, including payment schedules, responsibilities of each party, and the timeline for closing the deal.

Step 9: Financing

If you're financing the purchase, finalize your mortgage or financing arrangements. Foreigners can obtain financing from Philippine banks or international lenders, but this often requires substantial documentation and proof of income.

Step 10: Final Payment and Closing

The final step involves making the remaining payment as per the sales agreement, which can be through bank financing or personal funds. Upon payment, the Deed of Absolute Sale is signed by both parties, transferring ownership of the property.

Step 11: Transfer of Title

With the Deed of Absolute Sale signed, the next step is to transfer the title to the buyer's name. This involves paying the necessary taxes, like the capital gains tax, documentary stamp tax, transfer tax, and registration fees, then registering the sale with the Registry of Deeds.

Step 12: Move-in or Take Possession

Once the title transfer is completed and you've fulfilled all financial obligations, you can take possession of the property, move in, or begin any planned renovations or developments.

Key Considerations

- **Tax Implications**: Be aware of the tax implications and ongoing property taxes required by the Philippine government.
- **Insurance**: Consider purchasing property insurance to protect your investment against natural disasters, especially in areas prone to such events.
- **Maintenance and Management**: If you're buying property as an investment or second home, consider how it will be maintained or managed in your absence.

Conclusion

Buying property in the Philippines as a foreigner involves navigating a series of legal, financial, and practical steps. From understanding the restrictions on foreign ownership to engaging the right professionals, due diligence at every stage is key to a successful purchase. With careful planning, the right support, and adherence to legal processes, you can secure a property that meets your retirement needs, investment goals, or personal preferences, ensuring a rewarding experience in one of Southeast Asia's most living countries.

13 > Designing Your Home

Designing a home in the Philippines presents unique challenges and opportunities, given the country's tropical climate, cultural diversity, and evolving architectural territory. A well-designed home not just provides comfort and security but also reflects the owner's personality while being attuned to the environmental and social context of its location. This guide aims to cover the key considerations for designing a home in the Philippines, focusing on architectural styles, climate adaptability, and sustainable practices.

Understanding the Philippine Climate

The climate is a primary consideration in home design in the Philippines, characterized by hot, humid summers; a rainy season with potential typhoons; and a cooler, dry season. Effective designs incorporate features that address these conditions, ensuring comfort and durability.

- **Ventilation**: Good airflow is very important to maintain comfort in hot and humid conditions. Design homes with large windows, high ceilings, and open layouts to encourage natural ventilation.
- **Sunlight**: Utilize natural light while minimizing heat gain by positioning windows and overhangs strategically. Materials with reflective properties can also reduce heat absorption.
- **Insulation**: Proper insulation helps maintain a comfortable indoor temperature. Roof materials that reflect sunlight and walls constructed with insulating materials can significantly effect the home's thermal comfort.

Architectural Styles in the Philippines

The Philippines boasts an opulent architectural heritage, influenced by its history, culture, and adaptations to the tropical climate. Modern homes often blend traditional elements with contemporary designs, reflecting a fusion of influences.

- **Bahay Kubo/Nipa Hut**: The traditional Filipino house, known for its simplicity, elevated design, and use of local materials like bamboo and nipa palm. Its raised structure promotes airflow and protection from floods.
- **Bahay na Bato**: A style that evolved from the Bahay Kubo, incorporating stronger materials like wood and stone. It features the famous "ventanillas" (small windows below the main windows) and "capiz" shell windows.
- **Modern Tropical**: This style integrates modern architectural principles with tropical living elements, focusing on sustainability, open spaces, and indoor-outdoor living. Large glass windows, sustainable materials, and green spaces are common features.

Climate Adaptability and Sustainable Practices

Designing a home in the Philippines today requires a commitment to sustainability and resilience, especially in the face of climate change.

- **Eco-friendly Materials**: Use sustainable, locally sourced materials that reduce the environmental effect. Bamboo, reclaimed wood, and recycled materials are excellent choices for eco-conscious construction.
- **Water Conservation**: Implement rainwater harvesting systems and water-efficient fixtures to conserve water. Landscaping with native plants can also reduce water usage.
- **Energy Efficiency**: Consider solar panels to harness the abundant sunlight. Energy-efficient appliances and lighting can further reduce electricity consumption.
- **Disaster-Resilient Features**: Design homes to withstand natural disasters common in the Philippines, like typhoons

and earthquakes. Reinforced structures, flexible design elements, and strategic site selection are critical.

Integrating Outdoor and Indoor Spaces

The Philippine climate allows for a seamless blend of outdoor and indoor living spaces, enhancing the quality of life.

- **Lanais and Patios**: Incorporate covered outdoor areas that provide additional living space while protecting from the sun and rain.
- **Gardens and Green Spaces**: Design gardens and green areas around the home to improve air quality, provide natural cooling, and create a tranquil environment.
- **Natural Swimming Pools**: Consider eco-friendly natural swimming pools that use plants and natural processes to clean the water, offering a sustainable alternative to traditional pools.

Cultural Considerations and Personalization

Incorporating cultural elements and personal tastes makes a home truly reflective of its occupants.

- **Filipino Art and Craft**: Integrate Filipino art and craftsmanship to celebrate cultural heritage. Local textiles, wood carvings, and pottery can add character and warmth to the home.
- **Customization for Lifestyle**: Design spaces that cater to your lifestyle, whether it's a spacious kitchen for cooking enthusiasts, a home office for remote work, or a hobby room for arts and crafts.

Conclusion

Designing a home in the Philippines is an opportunity to create a space that is both personally meaningful and responsive to the local environment. By considering the climate, embracing a blend of architectural styles, prioritizing sustainability, and incorporating personal and cultural elements, you can design a home that offers comfort, functionality, and a deep connection to the Philippine setting.

The process requires careful planning, creativity, and an understanding of the unique challenges and opportunities presented by the tropical climate and opulent cultural territory of the Philippines.

14 > Navigating Construction

Embarking on a construction project in the Philippines entails navigating a comprehensive process that includes planning, securing permits, and executing the build itself. This complex adventure requires an understanding of local regulations, a careful selection of construction professionals, and an awareness of the unique environmental and logistical challenges present.

Initial Planning and Design

1. **Defining Project Scope and Objectives**: Begin by clearly outlining your construction project's scope, budget, and objectives. Consider factors like the purpose of the structure, desired features, and long-term plans.

2. **Hiring an Architect**: Engage a licensed architect to translate your vision into a feasible design. The architect will consider your requirements, the site's characteristics, and local building codes to develop preliminary designs and detailed plans.

Securing Construction Permits

3. **Understanding Required Permits**: Construction in the Philippines requires several permits from local government units (LGUs) and other regulatory bodies. Commonly required permits include a Building Permit, Barangay Clearance, and Environmental Compliance Certificate (ECC), among others.

4. **Preparing Documentation**: Application for permits involves compiling a comprehensive set of documents, including architectural plans, structural calculations, and site assessments. Your architect and engineer will hold very important roles in preparing these documents.

5. **Navigating the Permit Process**: Submit the permit applications to the relevant LGUs and agencies. This process can be time-consuming, requiring patience and occasional follow-ups. Engaging a professional with experience in local permit processes can streamline approvals.

Selecting a Construction Team

6. **Choosing a Contractor**: Selecting the right contractor is critical to your project's success. Look for licensed contractors with a good track record, transparent pricing, and strong references. Conduct interviews and review past projects to assess compatibility with your vision and standards.

7. **Vetting Subcontractors and Suppliers**: Your main contractor will likely engage subcontractors for specialized tasks. Ensure these entities are also vetted for quality and reliability. Similarly, scrutinize material suppliers to ensure the quality of construction materials.

8. **Contract Negotiation and Signing**: Once you've selected your contractor, negotiate the terms of the contract. This should include detailed specifications, timelines, payment schedules, and mechanisms for handling changes and disputes. Legal review of the contract is advisable before signing.

Construction Phase

9. **Site Preparation**: The first physical step involves preparing the construction site. This may include clearing land, setting up temporary utilities, and ensuring access for materials and equipment.

10. **Foundation and Structural Work**: The construction begins with laying the foundation, followed by the structural frame. These stages are critical for the building's integrity and must comply with architectural and engineering specifications.

11. **Mechanical, Electrical, and Plumbing (MEP) Installations**: Once the structure is in place, the installation of MEP systems begins. Coordination among different trades is essential to ensure that systems are installed efficiently and without conflicts.

12. **Finishing Works**: This phase covers everything from plastering and painting to the installation of fixtures and fittings. Quality control is very important to ensure finishes meet the design specifications and standards.

Oversight and Quality Control

13. **Regular Site Inspections**: Conduct regular inspections with your architect and engineer to monitor construction quality, adherence to plans, and compliance with safety standards. Address any issues promptly to prevent delays and cost overruns.

14. **Managing Changes**: Changes are common in construction projects. Ensure there's a clear process for reviewing, approving, and documenting changes, including their effect on costs and timelines.

Completion and Post-Construction

15. **Final Inspections and Certifications**: Upon completion, final inspections by the local building officials are required to obtain a Certificate of Occupancy. This certifies that the building complies with all codes and is safe for occupation.

16. **Settling Final Accounts**: Review and settle final accounts with the contractor, including any adjustments for changes or additional works.

17. **Maintenance and Warranty Period**: Post-construction, there's typically a warranty period during which the contractor is responsible for addressing any defects or issues that arise.

Conclusion

Navigating construction in the Philippines is a multifaceted process that demands attention to detail, adherence to legal requirements, and effective collaboration with professionals. By understanding each step, from initial planning and securing permits to construction and final inspection, you can ensure a smoother process and a quality finished project. Engaging reputable professionals, maintaining open communication, and staying involved throughout the project are key to overcoming challenges and achieving your construction goals.

15 > Utilities and Maintenance

Managing utilities and maintenance is a critical aspect of homeownership, especially in a new country where systems and processes might differ significantly from what one is accustomed to. In the Philippines, setting up utilities and ensuring their ongoing maintenance requires navigating local regulations, understanding the climate's effect on your home, and knowing who to contact for common issues.

Setting Up Utilities

Electricity: The Philippines' electricity sector is privatized, with distribution managed by local utility companies like Meralco in Metro Manila and other providers in different regions. To set up an electricity account:
1. Visit the local utility office with identification, proof of ownership or lease, and possibly a deposit.
2. Fill out an application form and submit the required documents.
3. Await inspection and meter installation, if necessary.

Water: Water supply is managed by local water districts or private companies. Similar to electricity, setting up water service involves:
1. Applying at the local water provider with necessary documentation.
2. Paying any applicable fees or deposits.
3. Coordinating any required inspections or installations.

Internet and Cable: The Philippines has several internet and cable providers, offering various packages. Research providers in your area to compare services and prices. Application can typically be done online or in service centers, requiring ID and proof of address. Installation schedules vary by provider.

Ongoing Maintenance

The tropical climate of the Philippines presents unique maintenance challenges, including high humidity, heavy rainfall, and potential for pests.

Regular Cleaning and Ventilation: Regularly clean your home to prevent mold and mildew growth caused by high humidity. Ensure adequate ventilation to keep indoor air fresh and reduce moisture.

Roof and Gutter Maintenance: Inspect your roof and gutters regularly, especially before the rainy season, to ensure they are in good condition and clear of debris to prevent leaks and water damage.

Pest Control: Termites, ants, and other pests can be a problem. Regular pest control treatments can help prevent infestations. Natural remedies or professional pest control services can address existing issues.

Air Conditioning Units: Given the climate, air conditioning is a common necessity. Regular servicing, including cleaning filters and checking coolant levels, is very important for efficiency and longevity.

Dealing with Common Issues

Power Outages: Power outages can be common, especially during typhoon season. Invest in surge protectors for sensitive electronics and consider backup power solutions like generators or UPS systems for critical needs.

Water Supply Issues: Water interruptions may occur, particularly in areas with limited supply. Large storage tanks and water pumps can mitigate these issues, ensuring a continuous water supply.

Internet Connectivity: Internet reliability can vary. Having a backup internet solution, like a mobile data plan, can keep you connected during service interruptions.

Structural Repairs: For structural issues or significant repairs, it's advisable to consult with a professional contractor or engineer to ensure repairs are done safely and up to code.

Tips for Effective Utility Management and Maintenance

Understand Your Bills: Familiarize yourself with how utility bills are structured and what charges to expect. This helps in monitoring usage and identifying any discrepancies.

Emergency Contacts: Keep a list of emergency contacts for utility services, maintenance providers, and local authorities for quick access in case of issues.

Community Resources: Engaging with local community groups or expatriate networks can provide valuable tips and recommendations for managing utilities and maintenance in your area.

Regular Check-ups: Schedule regular check-ups for your home's critical systems. Preventive maintenance can save time, money, and inconvenience in the long run.

Conclusion

Effectively managing utilities and home maintenance in the Philippines requires a proactive approach to setup, regular care, and prompt action when issues arise. Understanding local processes for utility setup, maintaining your home to address the challenges of the tropical climate, and knowing how to handle common problems can ensure a comfortable living environment. By staying informed, building relationships with local service providers, and leveraging community knowledge, expatriates can navigate the complexities of utilities and home maintenance successfully.

PART IV: LIVING IN THE PHILIPPINES

16 > Daily Life and Integration

Adjusting to daily life in a new country involves a series of adaptations to local customs, navigating the transportation system, understanding shopping nuances, and integrating into the community. The Philippines, with its opulent cultural atlas, bustling cities, and laid-back rural areas, offers a unique blend of experiences that can be both rewarding and challenging for expatriates.

Understanding Local Customs and Culture

The Philippines is known for its hospitality, strong family values, and festive spirit. Respect for elders, politeness, and a sense of community are deeply ingrained in Filipino culture.

- **Communication Style**: Filipinos often use non-verbal cues and indirect communication to convey messages and avoid confrontation. Understanding these subtleties can help in effective communication and relationship building.
- **Social Gatherings**: Being part of a community often involves attending social gatherings, celebrations, and participating in local festivities, which are great opportunities for integration.
- **Religious Practices**: With a predominantly Catholic population, religious practices hold a significant place in daily life. Showing respect for these practices and understanding their importance can aid in cultural adaptation.

Navigating Shopping and Markets

Shopping in the Philippines varies from modern malls in urban centers to local markets and sari-sari (small neighborhood) stores, offering a glimpse into the local way of life.

- **Malls**: The Philippines boasts some of the largest malls in Asia, providing a one-stop shop for groceries, clothing, electronics, and entertainment. Malls are also social hubs where families and friends gather.
- **Local Markets**: For fresh produce, meat, and seafood, local markets (palengke) offer variety and freshness at lower prices. Bargaining is common in markets, so don't hesitate to negotiate.
- **Sari-Sari Stores**: These small stores are essential for daily needs or quick purchases. They embody the communal spirit, serving as informal gathering spots for locals.

Transportation

Public transportation in the Philippines is diverse, including jeepneys, tricycles, buses, and taxis, alongside modern options like ride-hailing apps.

- **Jeepneys and Tricycles**: Famous to the Philippines, jeepneys and tricycles are ubiquitous in cities and rural areas, providing affordable short to medium-distance travel. Understanding routes can be challenging initially but offers a truly local experience.
- **Buses and Ferries**: For longer distances, buses and ferries connect major cities and islands. Booking tickets in advance is advisable, especially during peak travel seasons.
- **Ride-Hailing Apps**: Services like Grab provide a convenient and safer option for city travel, with transparent pricing and route information.

Daily Life Adaptations

- **Food and Cuisine**: Filipino cuisine is a blend of indigenous, Spanish, Chinese, and American influences. Embrac-

ing local dishes and ingredients can enrich your culinary experience and integration into local life.
- **Language**: While English is widely spoken, learning basic Filipino (Tagalog) phrases can greatly enhance daily interactions and show respect for the local culture.
- **Climate Adaptation**: The tropical climate necessitates adjustments in clothing, home ventilation, and daily routines, especially for staying hydrated and protecting against the sun.

Integration into the Community

- **Volunteering and Social Clubs**: Engaging in community service or joining clubs and organizations can provide meaningful connections and a sense of belonging.
- **Local Festivals and Events**: Participation in local festivals and events offers insights into Filipino heritage and builds community relationships.
- **Neighborhood Interaction**: Simple gestures like greeting neighbors and participating in local barangay (village) activities can open doors to deeper cultural immersion and acceptance.

Conclusion

Adapting to daily life in the Philippines is an adventure of cultural immersion, learning, and adaptation. Embracing the local customs, understanding the nuances of shopping and transportation, and actively seeking integration into the community can transform the expatriate experience from one of mere residence to a deeply enriching life among welcoming and living people. Patience, openness, and a willingness to learn and adapt are key to making the most of your new life in the Philippines, where every day can bring new discoveries and connections.

17 > Expat Communities and Networking

Engaging with expatriate communities and networking in a new country is an essential aspect of the relocation process, offering necessary support, valuable information, and opportunities for socializing. In the Philippines, a country known for its welcoming nature and living expat scene, connecting with fellow expatriates can greatly enhance your living experience.

Understanding the Place of Expat Communities

Expat communities act multiple roles, from providing a sense of belonging to offering practical advice on living and working in the Philippines. They can be a source of:
- **Information and Support**: Sharing experiences on navigating local bureaucracy, finding housing, and understanding cultural nuances.
- **Social and Professional Networking**: Opportunities to meet people in various fields, which can be beneficial for those looking to expand their professional contacts or simply make friends.
- **Cultural Exchange**: A platform to exchange cultural insights, which can enhance mutual understanding and integration.

Finding Expat Communities

Online Platforms: Websites and social media groups are invaluable for connecting with expat communities. Facebook groups, forums like Expat.com, and platforms like Internations offer committed spaces for expats in the Philippines to share advice, experiences, and organize meet-ups.

Local Clubs and Associations: Many cities in the Philippines host international clubs, chambers of commerce, and cultural associations that organize regular social events, business networking meetings, and cultural exchange programs.

Community Boards and Local Publications: Community bulletin boards in international schools, churches, and community centers often have information on expat gatherings and events. Local expat-focused publications and websites can also provide insights into community activities.

Embassies and Consulates: Foreign embassies and consulates sometimes hold events for their nationals or have information on local expat groups and activities.

Engaging with Expat Communities

Attend Events and Meet-ups: Actively participating in community events, social gatherings, and professional networking meet-ups is one of the most effective ways to engage with expat communities.

Volunteer: Volunteering for community service projects or events organized by expat groups not just contributes positively to your new home but also helps in making meaningful connections.

Start Your Own Group: If you have a specific interest or hobby that isn't represented, consider starting your own group. This can be a great way to meet like-minded individuals and contribute to the diversity of the expat community.

Language and Cultural Exchange: Participate in language and cultural exchange meet-ups. These can be beneficial in improving your language skills and understanding of Filipino culture, facilitating deeper integration.

Benefits of Engaging with Expat Communities

Cultural Adaptation: Expat communities can ease the transition into your new environment by helping you navigate cultural differences and avoid common pitfalls.

Emotional Support: Relocating can be challenging, and having a support network of people who have gone through similar experiences can provide emotional comfort and advice.

Local Insights: Beyond practical advice, engaging with expats can offer insights into local life, hidden gems, and experiences that might not be readily available through other channels.

Expanding Social Circles: Joining expat communities opens up opportunities to meet a diverse range of people, expanding your social and professional circles.

Challenges and Considerations

While expat communities offer numerous benefits, it's also important to strive for a balanced social life that includes local interactions. Engaging solely with expat groups can limit full cultural immersion and understanding of the Philippines. Efforts to learn the language, participate in local traditions, and build relationships with Filipinos will enrich your expatriate experience significantly.

Conclusion

Finding and engaging with expat communities in the Philippines is a valuable part of the expatriate adventure, providing support, information, and opportunities for socializing and professional networking. By leveraging online platforms, local clubs, and community events, expatriates can navigate their new environment more effectively and enrich their living experience. Balancing engagement with both expat and local communities ensures a well-rounded and fulfilling expatriate life in the living and diverse setting of the Philippines.

18 > Travel and Adventure within the Philippines

Traveling and exploring the Philippines offers a unique opportunity to immerse oneself in the country's stunning natural landscapes, opulent cultural heritage, and living local communities. From the pristine beaches of Palawan to the historic streets of Vigan, the Philippines is a treasure trove of experiences waiting to be discovered.

Preparing for Travel

Plan Ahead: Research your destinations to understand the best times to visit, cultural norms, and any local festivals or events. Booking accommodations and transportation in advance is recommended, especially during peak travel seasons.

Pack Accordingly: The tropical climate requires lightweight and breathable clothing, but also bring rain gear and warmer layers for higher elevations. Essentials include sunscreen, insect repellent, and a reusable water bottle.

Stay Healthy: Ensure you're up to date on vaccinations recommended for travel in the Philippines. Be mindful of food and water safety to avoid common travel-related illnesses.

Must-Visit Places

Palawan: Often dubbed the "Last Frontier," Palawan is renowned for its crystal-clear waters, limestone cliffs, and incredible biodiversity. Highlights include El Nido, Coron, and the Underground River in Puerto Princesa.

Boracay: After a six-month closure for rehabilitation, Boracay has reemerged as a more sustainable tourist destination. Its white sandy beaches and living nightlife continue to draw visitors from around the world.

Siargao: Known as the surfing capital of the Philippines, Siargao has much more to offer beyond its waves. Explore the natural beauty of the island through its lagoons, caves, and coconut palm forests.

Batanes: The northernmost province of the Philippines, Batanes is characterized by its rugged terrain, traditional Ivatan houses, and serene landscapes, offering a peaceful retreat from the hustle and bustle of city life.

Cebu: A blend of urban and natural attractions, Cebu boasts historical landmarks, delicious cuisine, and nearby islands with stunning waterfalls and beaches.

Sagada: Nestled in the Cordillera Mountains, Sagada is famous for its hanging coffins, cave systems, and the serene beauty of its landscapes.

Domestic Travel Tips

Local Transportation: Familiarize yourself with the various modes of transportation, including jeepneys, tricycles, and ferries. Renting a scooter can be an enjoyable way to explore smaller islands and rural areas.

Communication: While English is widely spoken, learning a few basic phrases in Filipino or the local dialect can enhance your travel experience and interactions with locals.

Cultural Sensitivity: Respect local customs and traditions. Dress modestly when visiting religious sites and ask for permission before taking photos of people.

Safety Precautions

Stay Informed: Keep abreast of local news and advisories, especially regarding weather conditions that may affect travel plans, like typhoons and volcanic activity.

Protect Your Belongings: Be mindful of your possessions in crowded places and use reputable transportation services to avoid scams.

Health and Safety: Drink bottled or filtered water, apply mosquito repellent regularly, and practice sun safety to protect against heat-related illnesses and mosquito-borne diseases.

Emergency Preparedness: Have a basic first-aid kit, know the local emergency numbers, and keep the address and contact information of your country's embassy or consulate handy.

Sustainable Travel Practices

Respect Natural Sites: Follow guidelines for responsible tourism, especially in protected areas, to minimize your environmental effect. Avoid single-use plastics, and support eco-friendly tours and accommodations.

Support Local Communities: Engage with the local economy by purchasing from small businesses, eating at local restaurants, and participating in community-based tourism initiatives.

Conclusion

Exploring the Philippines offers an enriching atlas of experiences, from its natural wonders and historical sites to the warmth and hospitality of its people. By planning ahead, respecting local cultures and environments, and taking necessary safety precautions, travelers can fully start to take in the beauty and diversity of this living archipelago. Whether you're seeking adventure, relaxation, or cultural immersion, the Philippines promises an adventure filled with unforgettable memories.

19 > Safety and Security

Ensuring personal safety and securing property are paramount concerns for anyone, especially expatriates adapting to life in a new country. The Philippines, with its diverse urban and rural landscapes, presents a unique set of safety considerations.

Understanding Safety Concerns in the Philippines

The Philippines is generally a safe country for residents and visitors, but like any destination, it has areas and situations where safety risks are elevated. Key concerns include petty crime, natural disasters, and, in certain regions, political unrest.

- **Petty Crime**: Urban areas, particularly in major cities like Manila and Cebu, can experience higher rates of petty crime like pickpocketing, scams, and theft. Tourist areas are often targeted, necessitating vigilance.
- **Natural Disasters**: The Philippines is prone to natural disasters, including typhoons, earthquakes, and volcanic eruptions. Awareness and preparedness are very important.
- **Political Unrest**: Certain regions, especially in parts of Mindanao, have been affected by political unrest and conflicts. Government travel advisories should be consulted to identify areas currently taken into consideration unsafe.

Areas to Exercise Caution

While it's important not to generalize or stigmatize any specific area, being informed about locations with heightened safety risks enables better decision-making.

- **Avoiding High-Risk Areas**: Stay informed about areas with travel advisories or warnings due to political instability or conflict.
- **Urban Safety**: In cities, be cautious in crowded places, public transport, and areas known for nightlife, as these can be hotspots for petty crimes.
- **Natural Disaster-Prone Areas**: Certain regions are more susceptible to natural disasters. If residing in or visiting these areas, understanding local emergency procedures and evacuation plans is essential.

Securing Your Home and Property

- **Choosing a Safe Location**: When selecting a residence, consider the area's overall safety, local crime rates, and proximity to emergency services.
- **Physical Security Measures**: Invest in robust locks, security doors, and, if necessary, window grilles. Security systems, including alarms and CCTV cameras, add an extra layer of protection.
- **Community Vigilance**: Engage with your local community or barangay (village) for mutual support. Neighborhood watch programs can enhance security for everyone.
- **Emergency Preparedness**: Have an emergency kit and plan in place, especially for natural disasters. This should include essential supplies, important documents, and an understanding of local emergency protocols.

Personal Safety Practices

- **Situational Awareness**: Always be aware of your surroundings and avoid displaying expensive items conspicuously.

- **Safe Transportation Choices**: Use reputable transportation services, especially at night. Be cautious with ride-sharing apps and verify the vehicle and driver before boarding.
- **Traveling Wisely**: Inform someone of your travel plans, especially if venturing to remote areas. Carry a charged mobile phone with emergency numbers saved.
- **Health Safety**: Be aware of health advisories, from water and food safety to precautions against mosquito-borne diseases.

Enhancing Security While Socializing and Traveling

- **Mindful Socializing**: Exercise caution when meeting new acquaintances and be mindful of your belongings in social settings.
- **Secure Travel Documents**: Keep your travel documents secure and have copies stored separately from the originals.
- **Insurance**: Ensure you have adequate insurance coverage for health, travel, and personal property. This provides an essential safety net.

Staying Informed

- **Local News:** Regularly follow local news and updates for any safety advisories or relevant information about your area.
- **Government and Embassy Updates**: Expatriates should register with their embassy or consulate and stay updated on any advisories or services offered.

Conclusion

Safety and security in the Philippines, as in any country, require a proactive approach centered on awareness, preparation, and engagement with the community. By understanding the specific risks, exercising caution in identified areas, and implementing measures to secure personal and property safety, expatriates and travelers can significantly mitigate risks and enjoy a rewarding experience in the Philippines. Cultivating a network of local contacts, staying informed about the local situation, and adopting a respectful understanding of cultural norms further enhance safety and contribute to a positive and secure living environment.

PART V: FINANCIAL MANAGEMENT

20 > Investment Opportunities

Investing in the Philippines presents a spectrum of opportunities for expatriates, driven by the country's growing economy, strategic location in Southeast Asia, and its emerging markets.

Real Estate Investment

1. **Residential and Commercial Properties**: The real estate market in the Philippines has shown resilience and growth, making it an attractive option for investors. While foreigners cannot own land directly, they can invest in condominium units, commercial spaces, or through real estate investment trusts (REITs).
- **Condominiums**: A popular choice due to the ease of ownership and potential rental income.
- **Commercial Real Estate**: Office spaces and retail outlets in business districts offer long-term lease income.
- **REITs**: These allow investors to enter the real estate market with less capital, offering income through dividends from managed real estate assets.

Stock Market

2. **Philippine Stock Exchange (PSE)**: Investing in stocks is an option for those looking to tap into the country's corporate growth.
- **Direct Stock Investment**: Buying shares of publicly listed companies through a broker.

- **Mutual Funds and Exchange-Traded Funds (ETFs)**: For those seeking diversified exposure without the need to manage individual stocks.

Business Ventures

3. **Starting a Business**: The Philippines encourages foreign investment in various sectors, but there are restrictions and specific areas where foreign ownership is limited or prohibited.
- Special Economic Zones (SEZs) and the Philippine Economic Zone Authority (PEZA) offer incentives for foreign investors in manufacturing, IT, and service sectors.
- **Retail and Franchise**: While there are restrictions on foreign ownership, franchising international brands or partnering with local entities can be viable routes.

Mutual Funds and Unit Investment Trust Funds (UITFs)

4. **Managed Investment Funds**: These provide an opportunity for expatriates to invest in a diversified portfolio managed by professionals.
- **Mutual Funds**: Invest in a mix of stocks, bonds, and other securities, managed by investment companies.
- **UITFs**: Offered by banks, these funds pool money from various investors to invest in a diversified portfolio.

Bonds and Fixed Income Securities

5. **Government and Corporate Bonds**: Investors looking for more stable investment options may consider bonds.
- **Government Securities**: Include treasury bills and bonds, taken into consideration low-risk investments.
- **Corporate Bonds**: Issued by private corporations, these may offer higher yields but come with increased risk.

Agricultural and Social Enterprises

6. **Agribusiness**: The Philippines' agricultural sector offers investment opportunities in organic farming, aquaculture, and high-value crops, often supported by government incentives.
- **Social Enterprises**: Investing in businesses that address social and environmental challenges can also yield returns while contributing to sustainable development.

Safety and Regulatory Considerations

- **Due Diligence**: Conduct thorough research or consult with professionals before making investment decisions.
- **Understanding Regulations**: Familiarize yourself with the legal and regulatory scaffolding governing foreign investment in the Philippines, including restrictions and reporting requirements.
- **Tax Implications**: Consider the tax implications of your investments, both locally and in your home country, to ensure compliance and optimize tax efficiency.

Conclusion

The Philippines offers a dynamic investment territory for expatriates, characterized by diverse opportunities ranging from real estate and the stock market to entrepreneurial ventures and managed funds. Successful investing in the Philippines requires a strategic approach, informed by thorough research, an understanding of the local regulatory environment, and careful financial planning. With the right approach and guidance, expatriates can capitalize on the growth potential of the Philippine market, achieving financial returns while contributing to the country's economic development. Engaging with local experts and financial advisors is very important to navigate the complexities of investing in a foreign market effectively.

21 > Protecting Against Scams

Protecting oneself against scams is a critical concern for expatriates worldwide, including those living in or considering moving to the Philippines. Expatriates can be particularly vulnerable to scams due to their unfamiliarity with local practices and legal systems.

Common Scams Targeting Expatriates

Real Estate Scams:
- **Fake Listings**: Scammers advertise non-existent properties or properties they don't own, often at attractive prices, to lure potential buyers or renters.
- **Title Fraud**: Selling property without clear or legitimate titles, leading to legal complications for the buyer.

Investment Scams:
- **Pyramid Schemes**: Promising high returns for recruiting others into a program rather than supplying investments or selling products.
- **High-Yield Investment Programs (HYIPs)**: Offering unsustainably high returns on investments, these schemes often collapse, leaving investors out of pocket.

Visa and Immigration Scams:
- **Fake Visa Services**: Offering guaranteed visas or expedited processing for a fee, these scammers provide fraudulent services or fail to deliver altogether.

- **Employment Scams**: Promising high-paying jobs abroad or in the Philippines, requiring payment for placement services, visas, or other fees, then disappearing once fees are paid.

Romance Scams:
- Developing online relationships and eventually asking for money for various emergencies, travel expenses, or medical bills.

Recognizing Scams

Too Good to Be True: Offers that seem too good to be true often are. High returns with no risk, properties significantly under market value, or jobs with unusually high salaries should raise red flags.

Pressure Tactics: Scammers often create a sense of urgency, pressuring you to make quick decisions or payments.

Request for Upfront Fees: Be cautious of any request for money upfront, especially if asked via wire transfer, gift cards, or other untraceable methods.

Lack of Transparency: Scammers avoid providing detailed information, valid contact details, or refuse to meet in person.

Unsolicited Offers: Unsolicited emails, calls, or messages offering investments, properties, or other opportunities are often scams.

Protecting Yourself from Scams

Do Your Research: Before making any financial commitments or personal information disclosures, thoroughly research the company, property, or individual. Use government and reputable industry websites to verify legitimacy.

Seek Professional Advice: Consult with legal professionals, real estate agents, or financial advisors, especially those with experience dealing with expatriates in the Philippines.

Secure Transactions: Ensure all transactions are documented and conducted through secure, traceable means. Avoid cash transactions for large payments.

Personal Information Security: Be cautious about sharing personal information, especially financial details, online or with strangers.

Educate Yourself: Familiarize yourself with common scams in the Philippines. Government websites, expatriate forums, and community groups can be valuable resources.

Trust Your Instincts: If something feels off, it likely is. Trust your instincts and seek advice or a second opinion if in doubt.

What to Do If You Encounter a Scam

Cease Communication: If you suspect a scam, cease all communication with the scammer immediately.

Report the Scam: Report the incident to local authorities, like the Philippine National Police (PNP) or the National Bureau of Investigation (NBI). Reporting can help prevent others from falling victim to the same scam.

Inform Your Embassy: Many embassies offer assistance or advice to their nationals who are victims of scams.

Spread Awareness: Sharing your experience in expatriate communities or forums can help raise awareness and prevent others from being scammed.

Conclusion

While the Philippines offers many opportunities for expatriates, it's very important to remain vigilant against scams. By recognizing common scams, practicing due diligence, and taking proactive steps for protection, expatriates can significantly reduce their risk of falling victim to fraudulent schemes. Education, awareness, and caution are key defenses against scams, ensuring a safe and positive experience in the Philippines.

22 > Estate Planning and Legal Affairs

Estate planning and managing legal affairs are very important for ensuring that your assets are distributed according to your wishes and that your loved ones are taken care of in your absence. For expatriates living in the Philippines, navigating the local legal system and understanding international implications make estate planning particularly complex.

Understanding the Legal Scaffolding

The Philippines' legal system has its own set of rules regarding estate planning, wills, and inheritance, influenced by civil law traditions. Key points include:

- **Civil Code of the Philippines**: Governs the laws on succession, wills, and inheritance, including the legal capacity to inherit, compulsory heirs, and the division of the estate.
- **Foreign Wills**: The Philippines recognizes foreign wills if they comply with the law of the country where they were executed, the law of the testator's nationality, or Philippine law.

Estate Planning Considerations for Expatriates

1. **Wills and Testaments**: Creating a will is fundamental to estate planning, ensuring your assets are distributed according to your wishes.

- **Choosing the Governing Law**: Expatriates should consider whether to create a will under Philippine law or the law of their home country, bearing in mind the recognition of foreign wills in the Philippines.
- **Naming an Executor**: Designate a trusted individual to execute the will, potentially someone familiar with both your home country's and Philippine legal systems.

2. **Real Property**: Special considerations apply to real estate, given restrictions on foreign ownership of land in the Philippines.

- **Condominium Units**: While expatriates can own condominium units outright, succession rules apply upon the owner's death, which may necessitate planning to ensure smooth transfer to heirs.
- **Land Ownership**: Since foreigners cannot own land, those who have acquired land through inheritance or other means must understand the legal processes for transferring or selling the property.

3. **Personal Property and Investments**: Other assets, including bank accounts, stocks, and personal property, should be included in estate planning.

- **Local and Offshore Accounts**: Understand the implications of holding assets in both the Philippines and abroad, including potential estate taxes and how they will be accessed by heirs.
- **Investment Vehicles**: Use of trusts, insurance policies, and investment accounts designated to beneficiaries can simplify the transfer of assets.

Legal Considerations for Expatriates

Immigration Status: Your residency status can affect estate planning, particularly regarding tax implications and the legal jurisdiction governing your estate.

Tax Implications: Be aware of estate tax obligations in the Philippines and potential tax liabilities in your home country.

Tax treaties may effect the taxation of estates for expatriates.

Healthcare Directives and Power of Attorney: Establishing durable powers of attorney for healthcare and financial decisions is essential, particularly for those who may spend extended periods in the Philippines.

Steps for Effective Estate Planning

1. **Consult with Legal Experts**: Engage attorneys familiar with both Philippine law and the legal system of your home country to navigate the complexities of international estate planning.
2. **Document Everything**: Ensure all documents, including wills, powers of attorney, and healthcare directives, are properly executed, witnessed, and stored in secure, accessible locations.
3. **Communicate with Family and Heirs**: Open discussions about your estate plan, where documents are stored, and your wishes can prevent confusion and conflict.
4. **Regularly Review and Update Your Plan**: Changes in personal circumstances, residency status, or laws necessitate regular updates to your estate plan to ensure its effectiveness.

Conclusion

Estate planning and managing legal affairs as an expatriate in the Philippines require careful consideration of local and international laws, thoughtful decision-making, and proactive planning. By understanding the legal scaffolding, considering the unique aspects of holding assets in the Philippines, and seeking expert advice, expatriates can ensure their estate is managed according to their wishes, providing peace of mind and security for themselves and their loved ones.

PART VI: HEALTH AND WELL-BEING

23 > Healthcare Services

Navigating the healthcare system in a new country can be daunting, especially for expatriates who are unfamiliar with local practices and standards. In the Philippines, a country known for its warm people and beautiful landscapes, healthcare services vary widely in terms of quality, accessibility, and cost across different regions. This guide aims to provide expatriates with comprehensive insights into accessing healthcare services, finding reputable doctors and hospitals, and understanding the nuances of the Philippine healthcare system.

Understanding the Philippine Healthcare System

The Philippine healthcare system is a mix of public and private healthcare providers. Public healthcare is accessible at lower costs, but facilities may be overcrowded and under-resourced, especially in rural areas. Private healthcare providers offer higher quality services with modern facilities and shorter waiting times but at a higher cost.

Public Healthcare: Administered by the Department of Health (DOH), public healthcare includes a network of hospitals, rural health units, and barangay (village) health centers. PhilHealth, the national health insurance program, provides coverage for a significant portion of healthcare costs for its members, including expatriates who choose to join.

Private Healthcare: Private hospitals and clinics are prevalent in urban areas and are preferred by most expatriates and those who can afford it for their higher standard of care. Top hospitals in Metro Manila, like St. Luke's Medical Center and Makati Medical Center, offer services comparable to Western countries.

Accessing Healthcare Services

PhilHealth Membership: Expatriates living and working in the Philippines can become voluntary members of PhilHealth. Registration requires submitting an application along with necessary documents and paying the premium. PhilHealth coverage can significantly reduce healthcare costs.

Private Health Insurance: Many expatriates opt for private health insurance, either purchased locally or through international providers. This insurance can cover services not fully covered by PhilHealth, including treatment in private hospitals, dental care, and medical evacuation.

Finding Doctors and Specialists: Personal recommendations from fellow expatriates, colleagues, or local friends are invaluable. Many doctors in urban centers received their education and training abroad and are fluent in English. Online directories and websites of major hospitals also list their medical staff with their specialties and credentials.

Tips for Navigating Healthcare in the Philippines

Scheduled Appointments: While walk-ins are common in some clinics, scheduling an appointment is recommended, especially with specialists, to reduce waiting times.

Medical Records: Keep a personal copy of your medical records, including previous treatments, allergies, and medications, which can be useful when consulting new healthcare providers.

Pharmacies: Pharmacies are widely available, including within malls and supermarkets. While many medications can be purchased over the counter, it's advisable to have a prescription for specific drugs, especially those that are regulated.

Emergency Services: In case of an emergency, private hospitals provide the highest quality of emergency care. It's important to know the nearest hospital with emergency services in your area. The Philippines does not have a unified emergency number, but 911 is being implemented in many areas as the standard emergency hotline.

Health Considerations in the Philippines

Vaccinations: Ensure routine vaccinations are up to date, and consult with a healthcare provider for recommended vaccines for living in the Philippines, like typhoid, hepatitis A and B, and rabies, depending on your area and lifestyle.

Environmental Health Risks: Be aware of environmental health risks, including dengue fever, malaria (in certain rural areas), and air pollution in urban centers. Taking preventive measures like using mosquito repellents and staying hydrated can mitigate these risks.

Healthcare for Chronic Conditions: If you have a chronic condition, research in advance to ensure continuity of care. This includes identifying specialists, availability of medications, and necessary adjustments to treatment plans.

Conclusion

For expatriates in the Philippines, effectively managing healthcare needs involves understanding the local healthcare system, securing adequate health insurance coverage, and establishing relationships with trusted healthcare providers. While the quality of healthcare can vary, the Philippines has many highly qualified doctors and well-equipped facilities, particularly in major urban centers. Proactive health management, including vaccinations and preventive care, and being informed about local health risks, ensure that expatriates can enjoy a healthy, fulfilling life in the Philippines.

24 > Wellness and Fitness

Maintaining health and fitness is a very important aspect of achieving a balanced and fulfilling lifestyle, especially for expatriates adjusting to life in a new country. The Philippines, with its opulent natural landscapes and growing urban wellness infrastructure, offers a wide array of opportunities for individuals to engage in physical activities, wellness practices, and healthy living.

Gyms and Fitness Centers

The Philippines has seen a surge in the popularity of gyms and fitness centers, ranging from local establishments to international franchises. Urban areas, in particular, host a variety of options:

- **Commercial Gyms**: Well-known chains like Anytime Fitness, Gold's Gym, and Fitness First offer extensive equipment, group classes, and personal training services across major cities.
- **Boutique Studios**: For those interested in specific workout regimes, boutique studios offering yoga, Pilates, spinning, and CrossFit are increasingly available, providing personalized experiences.
- **Community Centers and Sports Clubs**: Local barangay centers, sports clubs, and country clubs often have fitness facilities available to members and sometimes to the general public for a fee.

Outdoor Activities

The Philippines' diverse natural environment makes it an ideal location for outdoor fitness activities, offering both adventure and the chance to engage with the country's stunning landscapes:

- **Running and Cycling**: Many cities have developed parks and green spaces ideal for running and cycling. The UP Diliman campus in Quezon City, Bonifacio Global City in Taguig, and Iloilo River Esplanade are popular spots.
- **Hiking and Mountain Climbing**: The country's numerous mountains and trails provide opportunities for all levels of hikers and climbers. Destinations like Mt. Pulag, Mt. Pinatubo, and the trails of Rizal province offer breathtaking views and challenging treks.
- **Water Sports**: With over 7,000 islands, the Philippines is a haven for water sports enthusiasts. Activities like swimming, surfing, paddleboarding, and diving are widely accessible, especially in coastal areas like Siargao, La Union, and Palawan.

Wellness Centers and Spas

For those looking to focus on holistic wellness, the Philippines offers a variety of wellness centers and spas that incorporate traditional and modern healing practices:

- **Spas and Wellness Retreats**: Facilities offering massages, traditional Filipino hilot, and other therapeutic treatments are found throughout the country. Some, like The Farm at San Benito in Batangas, offer comprehensive wellness retreats.
- **Yoga and Meditation Centers**: Numerous centers offer yoga and meditation classes to help individuals maintain mental and physical health. These range from drop-in classes in city studios to immersive retreats in more secluded locations.

Healthy Eating

Maintaining a balanced diet is part of a comprehensive approach to wellness. The Philippines has a growing scene of health-conscious dining options:

- **Farm-to-Table Restaurants**: Establishments focusing on organic, locally sourced ingredients are becoming more common, especially in urban areas.
- **Healthy Eating Options**: Vegetarian and vegan restaurants, along with cafes offering healthy menus, cater to those looking for nutritious dining options.
- **Local Markets**: For those who prefer to cook at home, local markets provide access to fresh fruits, vegetables, and seafood. Organic farms and cooperatives also offer subscription boxes of fresh produce.

Community and Social Groups

Joining fitness-related social groups can provide motivation and enhance the expatriate experience:

- **Sports Leagues and Clubs**: Participating in local sports leagues or joining clubs for activities like tennis, golf, or martial arts can be a great way to stay active and meet new people.
- **Fitness and Wellness Events**: The Philippines hosts various events like marathons, triathlons, and yoga festivals, providing goals to work towards and opportunities to engage with the wider fitness community.

Conclusion

For expatriates in the Philippines, maintaining wellness and fitness can significantly enhance the quality of life, providing benefits that extend beyond physical health to include mental well-being and social engagement. The diverse opportunities available, from urban fitness centers and wellness retreats to outdoor adventures and healthy dining, mean that individuals can find activities that fit their interests and lifestyle. By exploring the various options and integrating fitness and wellness into their daily routines, expatriates can fully start to take in and enjoy their life in the Philippines, benefiting from the country's opulent culture and natural beauty.

25 > Diet and Nutrition

Adapting to local food and maintaining a healthy diet are significant aspects of the expatriate experience, especially in a country like the Philippines, where the cuisine is a living blend of flavors influenced by its diverse regions and historical connections. For expatriates, navigating the dietary territory involves discovering local culinary delights, sourcing familiar foods for comfort, and ensuring nutritional balance.

Understanding Filipino Cuisine

Filipino cuisine is characterized by its use of fresh ingredients, bold flavors, and a combination of sweet, sour, and salty tastes. Rice is a staple, served alongside a variety of dishes that include meat, seafood, vegetables, and fruits. Notable dishes include:

- **Adobo**: A marinated meat dish, typically chicken or pork, cooked in vinegar, soy sauce, garlic, and spices.
- **Sinigang**: A sour soup made with tamarind, meat (often pork, beef, or seafood), and various vegetables.
- **Lechon**: Roasted pig, known for its crispy skin and tender meat, often served on special occasions.

Adapting to Local Food

Exploring Local Markets and Street Food: Visiting local markets and trying street food are great ways to immerse yourself in Filipino food culture. Markets also offer fresh, local produce for home cooking.

Balanced Meals: While Filipino cuisine can be heavy on meat and sugar, it also offers a wide range of fresh fruits, vegetables, and seafood. Balance meals by incorporating these healthier options.

Cooking at Home: Learning to cook Filipino dishes at home allows for control over ingredients and portion sizes, making it easier to maintain a balanced diet.

Finding Familiar Foods

Supermarkets and Specialty Stores: Urban areas in the Philippines, especially Metro Manila, host supermarkets and specialty stores that carry imported goods and familiar brands from North America, Europe, and other Asian countries.

Online Shopping: E-commerce platforms and specialty online stores can be a convenient source for imported and specialty food items that are hard to find in local markets.

Health Food Stores: For those with specific dietary needs, health food stores and sections in larger supermarkets offer organic, vegan, vegetarian, and gluten-free options.

Maintaining a Healthy Diet

Incorporate Local Superfoods: The Philippines is opulent in "superfoods" like malunggay (moringa), kamote (sweet potato), and various tropical fruits (mango, papaya, and avocado) that are nutritious and can be easily included in your diet.

Hydration: Staying hydrated is very important in the tropical climate of the Philippines. Besides water, coconut water is a popular and healthy option for hydration and electrolytes.

Moderation with Sweets and Fried Foods: Filipino cuisine includes a variety of sweets and fried foods. Enjoy these in moderation while focusing on dishes prepared with fresh, whole ingredients.

Dietary Considerations

Eating Out: When dining out, look for restaurants that offer grilled, roasted, or steamed options as healthier alternatives to fried foods.

Allergies and Dietary Restrictions: If you have food allergies or dietary restrictions, learning key phrases in Filipino or the local dialect to communicate your needs can be helpful. Many restaurants are accommodating, but it's wise to explain your restrictions clearly.

Supplementation: Depending on your dietary needs and the availability of certain nutrients from local foods, you might consider supplements, especially for vitamins D and B12, calcium, and omega-3 fatty acids. Consulting with a healthcare provider is recommended.

Conclusion

Adapting to the local food environment in the Philippines while maintaining a healthy diet requires a mix of openness to new culinary experiences and mindfulness about nutritional balance. By exploring the richness of Filipino cuisine, making informed choices, and incorporating a variety of fresh local produce, expatriates can enjoy a healthy and enriching dietary experience. Finding a balance between savoring the flavors of local dishes and incorporating familiar and nutritious foods into your diet can contribute significantly to a satisfying and healthy expatriate life in the Philippines.

PART VII: CULTURAL AND SOCIAL INTEGRATION

26 > Engaging with the Local Community

Engaging with the local community in a new country is a rewarding experience that can enhance an expatriate's understanding of the local culture, facilitate meaningful connections, and contribute positively to their new home. In the Philippines, a country known for its hospitable and community-oriented culture, there are numerous ways for expatriates to get involved, from volunteer opportunities to cultural exchange programs.

Understanding Community Engagement

Community engagement in the Philippines goes beyond mere participation in local events; it's about building relationships, understanding the local way of life, and contributing to the community's welfare. It's an opportunity for expatriates to immerse themselves in Filipino culture, share their skills and experiences, and learn from the local populace.

Ways to Get Involved

Local Barangay Activities: The barangay, the smallest administrative division in the Philippines, often organizes community events, clean-up drives, and local celebrations. Participating in these activities can be a great introduction to community involvement.

Cultural Workshops and Classes: Enrolling in workshops or classes focused on Filipino culture, arts, crafts, or cooking can provide insights into the local heritage and open opportunities for interaction with like-minded individuals.

Language Exchange: Participating in language exchange meet-ups can help in learning Filipino or other regional languages, facilitating deeper connections with locals and understanding cultural nuances.

Volunteer Opportunities

Environmental Conservation: The Philippines is home to diverse ecosystems. Expatriates can volunteer for reforestation projects, marine conservation efforts, or wildlife protection programs with organizations like Haribon Foundation and the Philippine Reef and Rainforest Conservation Foundation.

Community Development: Engage in community development projects that focus on education, health, and livelihood. Organizations like Gawad Kalinga and the Philippine Red Cross offer various programs that welcome volunteers.

Teaching and Education: Share your knowledge by teaching English, computer skills, or other subjects. Non-profits like Teach for the Philippines seek volunteers to contribute to educational initiatives in underprivileged areas.

Cultural Exchange Programs

Cultural Immersion Programs: Participate in programs designed to immerse you in Filipino culture, including home stays, cultural tours, and traditional arts and crafts sessions.

International Cultural Festivals: Attend or volunteer at cultural festivals that celebrate both Filipino and international cultures. These events are platforms for cultural exchange and understanding.

Expatriate Organizations and Clubs: Join expatriate clubs or international organizations that often engage in cultural exchange activities, charity events, and community service, providing a blend of local and international perspectives.

Tips for Successful Community Engagement

Be Open and Respectful: Approach community engagement with an open mind and respect for local customs and traditions. Showing genuine interest and sensitivity to cultural differences can pave the way for meaningful interactions.

Start Small: Begin with small, manageable activities to gradually build your confidence and understanding of how you can best contribute to the community.

Network: Use social media, local community boards, and expatriate forums to find opportunities for involvement and connect with individuals and organizations active in community work.

Consistency is Key: Regular participation and commitment can help build lasting relationships and trust within the community, enhancing the effect of your involvement.

Learn the Language: While English is widely spoken in the Philippines, learning the local language or dialect can significantly enrich your engagement with the community and show your commitment to integrating into local life.

Conclusion

Engaging with the local community in the Philippines offers a pathway to a richer, more fulfilling expatriate experience. Through volunteer work, cultural exchange, and active participation in community activities, expatriates can deepen their understanding of Filipino culture, contribute positively to their new home, and forge lasting friendships. Whether it's protecting the country's natural beauty, contributing to community development, or participating in cultural exchanges, the opportunities for involvement are as diverse as the archipelago itself. Building connections with the local community not just aids in personal growth but also in creating a sense of belonging in the Philippines.

27 > Religion and Spiritual Life

The religious territory of the Philippines is both diverse and living, reflecting centuries of cultural exchanges and the Filipinos' deeply grounded spirituality. Predominantly Catholic due to Spanish colonial influence, the country also embraces a variety of other faiths, including Islam, Protestantism, Buddhism, and indigenous beliefs, creating an opulent atlas of religious and spiritual practices. This diversity offers expatriates numerous opportunities for spiritual engagement and adventure.

Catholicism

Catholicism is the dominant faith in the Philippines, with about 80% of the population identifying as Catholic. This ubiquitous faith is evident in the country's churches, festivals, and daily life.

- **Churches and Cathedrals**: The Philippines is home to many historic churches and cathedrals, some of which are UNESCO World Heritage Sites, like the San Agustin Church in Manila.
- **Festivals**: Religious festivals, or "fiestas," are central to Filipino culture, celebrating patron saints with processions, dances, and communal feasts. The Sinulog Festival in Cebu and the Feast of the Black Nazarene in Manila are among the most famous.
- **Spiritual Practices**: Attending Mass, novenas, and other religious observances offer expatriates opportunities to experience Filipino spirituality and community.

Islam

Islam is the second largest religion in the Philippines, primarily concentrated in the Mindanao region and the Sulu archipelago. The Islamic community, or the Moro people, have an opulent cultural heritage.

- **Mosques and Islamic Centers**: The Golden Mosque in Manila and the Grand Mosque in Cotabato City are significant Islamic sites. Expatriates can visit these places for worship or to learn about Islamic traditions in the Philippines.
- **Cultural Festivals**: Events like Eid al-Fitr and Eid al-Adha are celebrated with communal prayers, feasts, and charity, providing a glimpse into the Islamic way of life.

Protestantism and Other Christian Denominations

The Philippines has a significant number of Protestants and members of other Christian denominations, including Iglesia ni Cristo, Seventh-day Adventists, and various evangelical and Pentecostal churches.

- **Church Services and Community Activities**: Protestant churches offer services in English and Tagalog, bible study groups, and community outreach programs, welcoming expatriates to join.

Eastern Religions and Indigenous Beliefs

Buddhism, Hinduism, and indigenous Filipino spiritual practices are also part of the country's religious territory.

- **Temples and Cultural Centers**: Buddhist and Hindu temples in cities like Manila offer services and festivals. The Chinese-Filipino community celebrates traditional Chinese festivals, like Chinese New Year, with lion dances, fireworks, and offerings.

- **Indigenous Spiritual Practices**: Indigenous groups across the Philippines maintain ancestral spiritual traditions. Engaging with these communities can offer unique insights into the country's pre-colonial belief systems.

Opportunities for Spiritual Engagement

Interfaith Groups: Joining interfaith dialogues and groups can provide a platform for learning about different religions and engaging in spiritual discussions.

Volunteer Work: Many religious organizations in the Philippines are involved in social work, education, and healthcare. Volunteering offers a way to contribute to the community while exploring spiritual values.

Meditation and Retreat Centers: For those seeking peace and introspection, the Philippines has several meditation and retreat centers, including those offering silent retreats, yoga, and wellness programs.

Cultural Immersion: Participating in religious festivals and visiting sacred sites can deepen understanding of the Philippines' spiritual diversity and history.

Conclusion

The religious and spiritual territory of the Philippines offers expatriates an opulent field for adventure and engagement. Whether through participation in living festivals, attendance at religious services, or involvement in community and volunteer activities, expatriates have numerous opportunities to connect with the spiritual life of their new home. Engaging with the diverse religious practices in the Philippines not just enriches the expatriate experience but also encourages a deeper appreciation of the country's cultural and spiritual heritage.

28 > Learning and Hobbies

Embarking on an adventure of learning and pursuing hobbies in a new country can significantly enhance an expatriate's experience, offering opportunities for personal growth, cultural immersion, and social interaction. The Philippines, with its opulent cultural heritage and diverse natural territory, provides a fertile ground for a wide range of learning activities and hobbies. Whether it's diving into the Filipino language and culture, exploring the great outdoors, or engaging in artistic and culinary pursuits, the possibilities for enrichment are boundless.

Language Learning

Filipino and English: The Philippines is predominantly bilingual, with Filipino and English as official languages. Learning Filipino can greatly enhance daily interactions and deepen understanding of the local culture. Numerous language schools and tutors offer courses ranging from beginner to advanced levels. Additionally, engaging in language exchange meet-ups can provide practical speaking experience.

Regional Languages: The Philippines is home to over 170 languages. Expatriates residing in specific regions might find learning the local language (like Cebuano, Ilokano, or Waray) both challenging and rewarding, offering deeper insights into regional cultures.

Cultural Immersion and Arts

Traditional Crafts: The Philippines has an opulent tradition in crafts like weaving, pottery, and woodcarving. Workshops and classes are available for those interested in learning these skills from master artisans, often organized by cultural centers and local communities.

Dance and Music: Traditional Filipino dance and music reflect the country's diverse cultural influences. Joining dance groups or music classes can be a delightful way to engage with Filipino heritage and meet locals with similar interests.

Cooking Classes: Filipino cuisine's unique flavors can be explored through cooking classes that teach the preparation of traditional dishes. Such classes are not just educational but also a fun way to engage with Filipino culture and cuisine.

Outdoor and Recreational Activities

Diving and Snorkeling: The Philippines is renowned for its opulent marine biodiversity, making it a premier destination for diving and snorkeling. From beginners to certified divers, there are courses and excursions to explore the underwater world of the Philippine archipelago.

Hiking and Mountaineering: With its numerous mountains and volcanoes, the Philippines offers hiking opportunities for all levels of experience. Joining local hiking clubs or groups can provide guidance for safely exploring the country's natural landscapes.

Surfing and Water Sports: The Philippines' extensive coastline is ideal for surfing, paddleboarding, and other water sports. Many coastal areas offer lessons and equipment rentals for beginners and enthusiasts alike.

Volunteer Work and Community Service

Engaging in volunteer work is a fulfilling way to contribute to the community while residing in the Philippines.

Opportunities include environmental conservation projects, educational tutoring, and participation in community development programs. Organizations like the Philippine Red Cross, Gawad Kalinga, and various NGOs offer platforms for expatriates to get involved.

Educational Pursuits

Academic Courses: For those interested in academic advancement, the Philippines hosts several reputable universities and colleges offering courses in diverse fields. Short courses, workshops, and seminars are also available for continuing education and professional development.

Art and Photography: The scenic beauty and cultural diversity of the Philippines provide ample inspiration for artists and photographers. Workshops in painting, drawing, photography, and digital arts are widely available, catering to various skill levels.

Fitness and Wellness

Martial Arts: The Philippines is the birthplace of martial arts like Arnis, Eskrima, and Kali. Training in these traditional martial arts, or other disciplines like boxing, Muay Thai, and Brazilian Jiu-Jitsu, offers both physical conditioning and insight into Filipino martial traditions.

Yoga and Meditation: For those seeking wellness and mindfulness, yoga studios and meditation centers across the Philippines offer classes and retreats. These can be a great way to maintain physical health, mental well-being, and meet like-minded individuals.

PART VIII: LONG-TERM CONSIDERATIONS

29 > Renewal of Visas and Residency

Renewing visas and residency status in the Philippines is a very important process for expatriates to ensure their continuous legal stay in the country. The Philippines offers various types of visas and residency permits, each with specific renewal procedures mandated by the Bureau of Immigration (BI). Understanding these procedures, preparing the necessary documents, and adhering to deadlines is essential to avoid legal complications and ensure a smooth stay.

General Overview

Types of Visas and Residency:
- **Tourist Visa**: Often issued for 30 days upon arrival for many nationalities, with the possibility of extension.
- **Special Resident Retiree's Visa (SRRV)**: A non-immigrant visa offering indefinite stay with multiple entries and exits, aimed at retirees.
- **9(g) Pre-arranged Employment Visa**: For those employed in the Philippines, requiring sponsorship by the employer.
- **13(a) Non-Quota Immigrant Visa**: For foreign nationals married to a Filipino citizen, allowing for permanent residency.
- **Permanent Resident Visa**: Various categories exist, including those for former Filipino citizens and quota visas based on nationality.

Renewal Procedures

Tourist Visa Extensions:
- Tourist visas can be extended at any Bureau of Immigration office.
- Extensions are granted typically for 1, 2, or 6 months at a time, with a maximum stay of up to three years for most nationalities.
- Required documents usually include a duly filled application form, passport, current visa copy, and extension fees.

Special Resident Retiree's Visa (SRRV):
- SRRV holders need to check in with the Philippine Retirement Authority (PRA) annually.
- Renewal may involve presenting the SRRV ID, passport, and proof of the required time deposit maintenance in a Philippine bank.

9(g) Pre-arranged Employment Visa:
- Renewal involves coordination with the employer, who must file a petition for visa extension.
- Necessary documentation typically includes the employment contract, company sponsorship, BI Clearance Certificate, and payment of the visa fee.

13(a) Non-Quota Immigrant Visa and Permanent Resident Visa:
- Renewal often requires submission of the Annual Report to the BI within the first 60 days of the calendar year.
- Documents generally include the Alien Certificate of Registration Identity Card (ACR I-Card), proof of residency, and the report fee.

Dealing with Immigration

Timeliness: Submit renewal applications well before the expiry of the current visa or residency permit to avoid penalties or legal issues.

Documentation: Ensure all documents are complete, accurate, and up-to-date. Missing or incorrect documentation can delay the renewal process.

ACR I-Card: The Alien Certificate of Registration Identity Card is very important for foreign nationals in the Philippines and must be renewed separately from the visa or residency permit.

Immigration Compliance: Stay informed about any changes in immigration policies or requirements by regularly checking the Bureau of Immigration's official website or consulting with legal professionals specializing in immigration law.

Tips for a Smooth Renewal Process

Keep Records: Maintain organized records of all immigration documents, receipts, and official correspondences.

Legal Assistance: Consider hiring a legal advisor specializing in Philippine immigration law to navigate complex procedures or resolve issues.

Online Transactions: Take advantage of online platforms for appointments, application submissions, or fee payments where available to save time.

Stay Informed: Changes in immigration laws and procedures can occur; staying informed through official channels is very important.

Conclusion

Renewing visas and residency status in the Philippines requires careful attention to detail, adherence to the procedures set by the Bureau of Immigration, and timely action. By understanding the specific requirements for their visa or residency type, preparing the necessary documentation, and following the proper channels, expatriates can ensure their legal status in the Philippines is maintained without interruption. Engaging with the process proactively,

seeking professional advice when needed, and staying informed about any legal changes are key to navigating the
complexities of immigration and residency renewal successfully.

30 > Planning for the Unexpected

Living in a new country entails facing a spectrum of unforeseen challenges, from personal emergencies and health crises to natural disasters, especially in a country as geographically and climatically diverse as the Philippines. Known for its natural beauty, the Philippines is also prone to various natural disasters, including typhoons, earthquakes, and volcanic eruptions. For expatriates, preparing for the unexpected is very important to ensure safety, minimize disruption, and navigate the complexities of an emergency in a foreign context.

Understanding the Risks

Natural Disasters: Familiarize yourself with the types of natural disasters common in the Philippines and the specific risks in your area. Key concerns include:
- **Typhoons**: The Philippines is hit by an average of 20 typhoons a year, some of which can cause significant damage.
- **Earthquakes**: The country is located on the Pacific "Ring of Fire" and experiences frequent seismic activity.
- **Volcanic Eruptions**: With several active volcanoes, including Mount Mayon and Taal Volcano, eruptions can pose threats to nearby areas.

Health Emergencies: Understanding the local healthcare system and having a plan for medical emergencies is essential. This includes knowing the nearest hospitals, emergency numbers, and having adequate health insurance.

Political and Social Unrest: While generally stable, the Philippines can experience political demonstrations. Staying informed about the local political climate and avoiding demonstrations can reduce risks.

Emergency Preparedness

Emergency Kits: Prepare emergency kits for your home and vehicle, including basic supplies like water, non-perishable food, first-aid items, flashlights, batteries, and essential documents.

Communication Plans: Establish a communication plan with family, friends, and colleagues. This should include emergency contact numbers and a protocol for checking in during a disaster.

Evacuation Plans: Know the evacuation routes and procedures for your area, especially if living near known disaster-prone zones. Familiarize yourself with local government and community evacuation plans.

Insurance: Ensure you have comprehensive insurance coverage that includes natural disasters. Understand your policy details, including how to file claims.

Health and Safety

Medical Preparedness: Keep a list of essential medications and medical supplies. Know where to find medical assistance, including hospitals that cater to expatriates or have English-speaking staff.

Safety Measures at Home: Secure heavy furniture and appliances to prevent injury during earthquakes. Know how to turn off utilities like gas, water, and electricity in emergencies.

Staying Informed: Subscribe to alert services or follow local news and weather reports to stay updated on potential emergencies. The Philippine Atmospheric, Geophysical, and Astronomical Services Administration (PAGASA) provides weather updates and warnings.

Building Local Networks

Community Engagement: Engaging with your local community can provide support and valuable information during emergencies. Community groups often have systems in place for assisting members in distress.

Embassy Registration: Register with your home country's embassy or consulate upon arrival in the Philippines. Embassies can provide assistance to their nationals during emergencies.

Legal and Financial Preparedness

Important Documents: Keep copies of important documents (passport, visa, insurance policies, medical records) in a secure and easily accessible location. Consider having digital copies stored securely online.

Financial Reserves: Maintain an emergency fund that can cover unexpected expenses, like medical emergencies or the need for sudden travel.

Mental Health and Resilience

Stress Management: Emergencies can be stressful. Develop strategies for managing stress, like maintaining a support network, practicing mindfulness, or seeking professional support if needed.

Adaptability: Being adaptable and maintaining a positive outlook can significantly effect your ability to cope with unexpected challenges. Learning from each experience strengthens resilience.

Conclusion

For expatriates in the Philippines, preparing for the unexpected involves a multifaceted approach encompassing understanding local risks, establishing practical preparedness measures, and building networks for support. By taking proactive steps to prepare for natural disasters, health emergencies, and other unforeseen challenges, expatriates can enhance their safety and well-being, ensuring a more secure and enriching experience in the Philippines. Adaptability, informed preparation, and community engagement are key to navigating the complexities of living in a dynamic and sometimes unpredictable environment.

31 > Reflections and Advice from Expatriates

Living as an expatriate in the Philippines offers a unique set of experiences, challenges, and rewards. The insights and advice from those who have navigated this adventure can provide invaluable guidance for others considering or preparing for retirement in this living country.

Embracing the Culture

Cultural Immersion: Expatriates focus on the importance of embracing Filipino culture with an open heart and mind. Learning about the country's history, traditions, and customs can enrich the expatriate experience and facilitate deeper connections with locals.

Language Learning: As mentioned previously, while English is widely spoken, learning Filipino or the local dialect of your area can significantly enhance daily interactions and show respect for the local culture. Language barriers can sometimes lead to misunderstandings, but making an effort to communicate in the local language is always appreciated.

Building Community

Local and Expat Communities: Successful expatriates often strike a balance between integrating into the local community and connecting with fellow expatriates. Participating in community events, volunteering, and joining clubs or groups can provide a sense of belonging and support.

Networking: Building a network of friends, acquaintances, and professional contacts is very important for navigating life in the Philippines. Networks can provide practical advice, emotional support, and enrich the social aspects of expatriate life.

Navigating Challenges

Adjusting Expectations: Life in the Philippines can differ significantly from expatriates' home countries. Adjusting expectations regarding time, convenience, and efficiency is often necessary. Patience and flexibility are key to overcoming day-to-day challenges.

Healthcare: Access to quality healthcare is a concern for many expatriates. It's advised to research healthcare facilities, secure comprehensive health insurance, and consider proximity to reputable hospitals when choosing where to live.

Legal and Financial Planning: Understanding the legalities of visas, property ownership, and taxation, and planning accordingly, is very important. Expatriates recommend consulting with legal and financial experts to navigate these complexities.

Enjoying the Lifestyle

Cost of Living: Many expatriates find the cost of living in the Philippines to be affordable, allowing for a comfortable lifestyle. However, budgeting wisely and being mindful of expenses is important to maintain financial health.

Natural Beauty and Travel: The Philippines is renowned for its natural beauty, from pristine beaches to lush mountains. Expatriates encourage exploring the diverse landscapes and destinations the country has to offer.

Safety: While the Philippines is generally welcoming and safe, like any country, it has areas of concern. Expatriates advise staying informed about local safety issues and taking common-sense precautions.

Personal Growth and Reflections

Cultural Sensitivity and Respect: Successful expatriates often speak of the importance of cultural sensitivity and respect. Understanding and honoring local ways of life can lead to a more harmonious and fulfilling experience.

Personal Growth: Many expatriates reflect on the personal growth experienced through their adventure, from learning to adapt to new situations to overcoming challenges and discovering new aspects of themselves.

Gratitude: Reflecting on their time in the Philippines, expatriates frequently express gratitude for the warmth and hospitality of the Filipino people, the friendships formed, and the experiences that have enriched their lives.

Conclusion

Retiring in the Philippines as an expatriate offers an adventure full of discovery, challenges, and rewards. The advice and reflections from those who have successfully navigated this path underscore the importance of openness, preparation, and community engagement. By embracing the local culture, building strong networks, and approaching life in the Philippines with flexibility and respect, expatriates can create a rewarding and enriching retirement experience. The shared wisdom of these expatriates acts as a valuable guide for those considering or embarking on their retirement adventure in the Philippines.

CONCLUSION

32 > Embracing Your New Life

Retiring in the Philippines offers a unique blend of opportunities, challenges, and adventures that can significantly enrich one's life in the golden years. With its stunning natural landscapes, living culture, and warm hospitality, the Philippines has become a sought-after retirement destination for many expatriates. However, embracing this new chapter involves more than just enjoying the scenic views and lower cost of living; it's about adapting to change, integrating into a new culture, and actively engaging in the community to make the most of the retirement experience.

Understanding and Adapting to Change

Cultural Adaptation: The first step to embracing your new life is understanding and adapting to the local culture. This means appreciating Filipino customs, traditions, and social norms. Efforts to learn the language, even basic phrases, can significantly enhance daily interactions and show respect for the local culture.

Managing Expectations: Life in the Philippines can present various challenges, from navigating bureaucratic processes to adjusting to the tropical climate. Setting realistic expectations and adopting a flexible attitude are very important for a smooth transition.

Staying Open to New Experiences: Retirement in the Philippines is an opportunity to explore new hobbies, interests, and activities. Whether it's diving into the local cuisine, exploring the islands, or participating in community events, staying open to new experiences can lead to personal growth and fulfillment.

Building a Supportive Community

Connecting with Fellow Expatriates: While integrating into the local culture is important, connecting with fellow expatriates can provide a sense of familiarity and mutual support. Expatriate groups and clubs can be valuable resources for advice, friendship, and social activities.

Engaging with the Local Community: Building relationships with locals can enrich your retirement experience immeasurably. Volunteer work, joining local clubs, or participating in barangay activities can facilitate cultural exchange and deeper connections.

Maintaining Connections Back Home: Keeping in touch with family and friends in your home country is also important. Modern technology offers various ways to stay connected, helping to balance your new life in the Philippines with relationships back home.

Prioritizing Health and Well-being

Access to Healthcare: Understanding the healthcare system and ensuring access to quality medical care are essential. This includes choosing a location with reputable healthcare facilities and securing comprehensive health insurance.

Physical Activity and Nutrition: The Philippines' natural environment offers numerous opportunities for physical activity, from swimming and hiking to yoga and golf. Embracing a diet opulent in local fruits, vegetables, and seafood can also contribute to overall well-being.

Mental Health: Adapting to a new life can be stressful. Prioritizing mental health through activities like meditation, hobbies, or seeking support from professionals or peer groups can enhance your quality of life.

Embracing the Adventure Ahead

Continuous Learning: Retirement in the Philippines is an ongoing adventure of learning and discovery. From understanding the country's history to exploring its diverse regions, there's always something new to learn.

Giving Back: Many expatriates find fulfillment in giving back to their new community, whether through teaching, environmental conservation, or supporting local charities. Such contributions not just make a positive effect but also add meaning and purpose to retirement life.

Reflecting and Documenting: Keeping a journal or blog about your retirement adventures, challenges, and reflections can be a rewarding way to document your adventure. It's also a way to share your experiences with others and act as a resource for future expatriates.

Conclusion

Embracing retirement in the Philippines is about more than just enjoying the beautiful surroundings and lower cost of living; it's an extremely significant adventure of adaptation, learning, and community engagement. By embracing change, staying open to new experiences, building a supportive network, and prioritizing health and well-being, expatriates can make the most of their retirement in the Philippines. This chapter of life offers a unique opportunity to explore, grow, and contribute in ways that are both personally fulfilling and enriching to the wider community. With the right approach and mindset, retirement in the Philippines can be a living and rewarding adventure.

33 > A Thank You

A Heartfelt Thank You from Phil Lipine -

As I sit down to pen this message, my heart is filled with an immense sense of gratitude. Reflecting on my adventure of retirement in the Philippines, I am overwhelmed by the beauty, kindness, and lessons this country has bestowed upon me. This thank you is more than a mere expression of gratitude; it is a celebration of the experiences, connections, and revelations that have shaped my life in extremely significant ways.

To the People of the Philippines,

Your warmth and hospitality are the soul of this beautiful country. From the moment I arrived, I was embraced with open arms and smiles that lit up even the rainiest days. Your generosity, resilience, and spirit of community have taught me invaluable lessons about kindness, strength, and the importance of togetherness. To every person who has shared a story, a meal, or a piece of advice, thank you for enriching my life and making me feel at home.

To the Expatriate Community,

Thank you for being my extended family away from home. Navigating the challenges and joys of expatriate life would have been a solitary adventure without your support and camaraderie. Our shared experiences, laughter, and mutual support have been pillars of strength and sources of joy. I am grateful for the friendships that have blossomed, for they are treasures I hold dear.

To the Culture and Traditions of the Philippines,

Embracing your opulent heritage has been an adventure of discovery. From the living festivals and the extremely significant religious devotion to the intricate dances and the exquisite cuisine, every aspect of Filipino culture has added color and depth to my life. Thank you for allowing me to partake in your traditions, learn from your history, and celebrate your achievements. These experiences have not just broadened my horizons but have also deepened my appreciation for the diversity and vibrancy of humanity's cultures.

To the Natural Wonders of the Philippines,

Your islands, seas, mountains, and skies have been a constant source of inspiration and tranquility. Exploring your breathtaking landscapes, from the serene beaches of Palawan to the majestic rice terraces of Banaue, has been a privilege. Thank you for the adventures, the sunsets, and the moments of awe that have reminded me of the beauty and majesty of our planet.

To the Lessons Learned and Growth Experienced,

This adventure has been one of personal evolution, marked by challenges overcome and insights gained. Thank you for the opportunities to learn, adapt, and grow. Each obstacle surmounted and every milestone achieved has been a step towards a richer, more fulfilled life.

In Conclusion,

My retirement in the Philippines has been an adventure of a lifetime, filled with moments that have touched my heart and shaped my soul. As I look forward to the adventure ahead, I carry with me an extremely significant sense of gratitude for the experiences that have been and an eager anticipation for those yet to come. To everyone who has been a part of this adventure, *maraming salamat po* (thank you very much).

With heartfelt thanks,

Phil Lipine

APPENDICES

Appendix A: Checklist for Retiring in the Philippines

This checklist covers pre-departure preparations, legal and financial arrangements, healthcare, housing, and community integration, aiming to address the key considerations for a successful retirement in the archipelago.

Pre-Departure Preparations

1. **Research**: Understand the Philippines' climate, culture, cost of living, and expatriate communities. Websites, forums, and blogs can offer valuable insights.
2. **Visit:** If possible, visit the Philippines before retiring to explore potential places to live and familiarize yourself with the local environment and lifestyle.
3. **Language**: Learn basic Filipino phrases and common expressions. English is widely spoken, but local language skills can enhance daily interactions.

Legal and Financial Arrangements

4. **Retirement Visa**: Research the best visa option for your situation. The Special Resident Retiree's Visa (SRRV) is popular among retirees for its benefits and ease of application.
5. **Banking**: Set up a local bank account and understand the procedures for transferring funds internationally. Consider currency exchange rates and fees.

6. **Insurance**: Secure comprehensive health insurance that covers medical care in the Philippines. Explore options for property and vehicle insurance if applicable.

7. **Legal Documentation**: Ensure your passport, visa, and other important documents are valid and accessible. Consider making digital copies stored securely online.

8. **Estate Planning**: Consult with a legal advisor to understand the Philippines' laws on wills and estates for expatriates. Consider how your plans affect your tax obligations.

Healthcare

9. **Healthcare Facilities**: Research hospitals and clinics, especially those near your intended place of residence. Check for English-speaking staff and available specialties.

10. **Medications**: Verify the availability of your prescription medications in the Philippines and understand the process for refilling prescriptions.

Housing

11. **Location**: Choose a location that aligns with your lifestyle preferences, whether it's a bustling city, a tranquil beach town, or a cooler climate in the mountains.

12. **Housing Options**: Decide whether to rent or buy. Research the real estate market, visit properties, and understand the legalities of property ownership for foreigners.

13. **Utilities Setup**: Learn about setting up electricity, water, internet, and other essential services. Prepare for possible initial deposits and setup fees.

Community Integration

14. **Social Networks**: Join expatriate groups, clubs, or organizations to meet people with similar interests and experiences.

15. **Volunteering**: Look for volunteer opportunities as a way to give back to the community and make meaningful connections.

16. **Cultural Engagement**: Participate in local festivals, events, and classes to immerse yourself in Filipino culture and history.

Daily Living

17. **Transportation**: Understand the local transportation options, like jeepneys, tricycles, taxis, and ride-sharing services. Consider obtaining a Philippine driver's license if you plan to drive.
18. **Communication**: Set up a local mobile phone plan for easy communication. Explore options for international calling and data plans.
19. **Groceries and Dining**: Familiarize yourself with local markets, grocery stores, and dining options. Experiment with local ingredients and cuisine.

Emergency Preparedness

20. **Emergency Contacts**: Compile a list of emergency contacts, including local emergency services, your embassy, healthcare providers, and close friends or family.
21. **Natural Disaster Preparedness**: Understand the protocols for typhoons, earthquakes, and other natural disasters common in the Philippines. Prepare an emergency kit with essential supplies.

Reflection and Adjustment

22. **Patience and Flexibility**: Be prepared for a period of adjustment and keep an open mind to the differences in culture and lifestyle.
23. **Continuous Learning**: Stay curious and open to learning, whether it's about the Filipino way of life, language, or exploring new parts of the country.

Conclusion

Retiring in the Philippines requires thorough preparation, from legal and financial arrangements to healthcare and community engagement. This checklist acts as a starting point for planning a successful and fulfilling retirement in the Philippines, emphasizing the importance of research, planning, and flexibility. By addressing these key considerations, expatriates can look forward to a rewarding retirement experience, embracing the beauty, culture, and warmth of the Philippines.

Appendix B: Useful Contacts and Resources

This checklist covers pre-departure preparations, legal and financial arrangements, healthcare, housing, and community integration, aiming to address the key considerations for a successful retirement in the archipelago.

Pre-Departure Preparations

1. **Research**: Understand the Philippines' climate, culture, cost of living, and expatriate communities. Websites, forums, and blogs can offer valuable insights.
2. **Visit:** If possible, visit the Philippines before retiring to explore potential places to live and familiarize yourself with the local environment and lifestyle.
3. **Language**: Learn basic Filipino phrases and common expressions. English is widely spoken, but local language skills can enhance daily interactions.

Legal and Financial Arrangements

4. **Retirement Visa**: Research the best visa option for your situation. The Special Resident Retiree's Visa (SRRV) is popular among retirees for its benefits and ease of application.
5. **Banking**: Set up a local bank account and understand the procedures for transferring funds internationally. Consider currency exchange rates and fees.

6. **Insurance**: Secure comprehensive health insurance that covers medical care in the Philippines. Explore options for property and vehicle insurance if applicable.

7. **Legal Documentation**: Ensure your passport, visa, and other important documents are valid and accessible. Consider making digital copies stored securely online.

8. **Estate Planning**: Consult with a legal advisor to understand the Philippines' laws on wills and estates for expatriates. Consider how your plans affect your tax obligations.

Healthcare

9. **Healthcare Facilities**: Research hospitals and clinics, especially those near your intended place of residence. Check for English-speaking staff and available specialties.

10. **Medications**: Verify the availability of your prescription medications in the Philippines and understand the process for refilling prescriptions.

Housing

11. **Location**: Choose a location that aligns with your lifestyle preferences, whether it's a bustling city, a tranquil beach town, or a cooler climate in the mountains.

12. **Housing Options**: Decide whether to rent or buy. Research the real estate market, visit properties, and understand the legalities of property ownership for foreigners.

13. **Utilities Setup**: Learn about setting up electricity, water, internet, and other essential services. Prepare for possible initial deposits and setup fees.

Community Integration

14. **Social Networks**: Join expatriate groups, clubs, or organizations to meet people with similar interests and experiences.

15. **Volunteering**: Look for volunteer opportunities as a way to give back to the community and make meaningful connections.

16. **Cultural Engagement:** Participate in local festivals, events, and classes to immerse yourself in Filipino culture and history.

Daily Living

17. **Transportation**: Understand the local transportation options, like jeepneys, tricycles, taxis, and ride-sharing services. Consider obtaining a Philippine driver's license if you plan to drive.
18. **Communication**: Set up a local mobile phone plan for easy communication. Explore options for international calling and data plans.
19. **Groceries and Dining**: Familiarize yourself with local markets, grocery stores, and dining options. Experiment with local ingredients and cuisine.

Emergency Preparedness

20. **Emergency Contacts**: Compile a list of emergency contacts, including local emergency services, your embassy, healthcare providers, and close friends or family.
21. **Natural Disaster Preparedness**: Understand the protocols for typhoons, earthquakes, and other natural disasters common in the Philippines. Prepare an emergency kit with essential supplies.

Reflection and Adjustment

22. **Patience and Flexibility**: Be prepared for a period of adjustment and keep an open mind to the differences in culture and lifestyle.
23. **Continuous Learning**: Stay curious and open to learning, whether it's about the Filipino way of life, language, or exploring new parts of the country.

Conclusion

Retiring In the Philippines requires thorough preparation, from legal and financial arrangements to healthcare and community engagement. This checklist acts as a starting point for planning a successful and fulfilling retirement in the Philippines, emphasizing the importance of research, planning, and flexibility. By addressing these key considerations, expatriates can look forward to a rewarding retirement experience, embracing the beauty, culture, and warmth of the Philippines.

Appendix C: Glossary of Terms and Phrases

This glossary aims to enhance understanding, facilitate smoother communication, and enrich the expatriate experience in the Philippines.

Legal and Immigration Terms

1. **ACR I-Card (Alien Certificate of Registration Identity Card)**: An identification card issued to foreign nationals registered under the Bureau of Immigration, serving as proof of their legal status in the Philippines.
2. **Balikbayan**: A Filipino returning to the Philippines after spending time abroad or a foreign spouse/child traveling with them. The term also refers to a privilege allowing Filipinos and their families visa-free entry for a year.
3. **Barangay**: The smallest administrative division in the Philippines, akin to a village or neighborhood.
4. **BI (Bureau of Immigration)**: The government agency responsible for regulating the entry, stay, and exit of foreigners in the country.
5. **Dual Citizenship**: The status of being a citizen of two countries simultaneously, recognized under Philippine law for former Filipino citizens and their descendants under certain conditions.
6. **NBI Clearance**: A government-issued document by the National Bureau of Investigation that certifies an individual has no criminal record in the Philippines.

7. **PhilHealth**: The national health insurance program of the Philippines, offering medical coverage to Filipino citizens and eligible foreigners.

8. **SRRV (Special Resident Retiree's Visa)**: A visa program offering indefinite stay with multiple entry and exit privileges to foreign retirees in the Philippines.

Cultural and Social Terms

9. **Bayanihan**: The spirit of communal unity and cooperation to achieve a particular goal, reflecting the Filipino value of helping one another.

10. **Fiesta**: A local festival celebrating a patron saint or important local event, characterized by parades, food, and various festivities.

11. **Jeepney**: A popular mode of public transportation in the Philippines, originally made from U.S. military jeeps left over from World War II.

12. **Kamusta**: A common greeting meaning "How are you?".

13. **Poblacion**: Refers to the town center or the downtown area where the municipal building, church, and plaza are located.

14. **Salamat**: Thank you.

15. **Pasalubong**: A gift or souvenir given by someone returning from a trip, reflecting the Filipino culture of generosity and thoughtfulness.

Food and Dining

16. **Adobo**: A popular Filipino dish made with meat (usually chicken or pork) marinated in vinegar, soy sauce, garlic, and spices.

17. **Halo-halo**: A cold dessert that includes shaved ice, evaporated milk, and various ingredients like sweet beans, coconut, sago, fruits, and ice cream.

18. **Lechon**: A whole roasted pig, often served during special occasions and celebrations.

19. **Sinigang**: A sour soup or stew characterized by its tamarind-based broth, with various meat and vegetables.

20. **Turo-turo**: Literally meaning "point-point," a type of eatery where customers point to the food they wish to order from an array of pre-cooked dishes.

Practical Phrases for Daily Use

21. **Magkano ito?**: How much is this?
22. **Saan ang CR?**: Where is the bathroom?
23. **Paumanhin**: Excuse me.
24. **Pwede ba akong tumulong?**: Can I help?
25. **Nasaan ang...?**: Where is...?

Emergency and Health

26. **Tulong!**: Help!
27. **May sakit ako**: I am sick.
28. **Saan ang ospital?**: Where is the hospital?
29. **Emergency:** Used in English, universally understood in the Philippines for urgent situations.
30. **Pulis:** Police.

Transportation and Directions

31. **Kaliwa:** Left.
32. **Kanan:** Right.
33. **Derecho**: Straight.
34. **Paano pumunta sa...?**: How to go to...?
35. **Sakay**: To ride; also used to refer to getting on public transportation.

Miscellaneous

36. **Mabuhay**: A traditional Filipino greeting meaning "live" or "long live", often used to welcome guests.
37. **Karaoke/Videoke**: A popular form of entertainment in the Philippines, involving singing along to lyrics displayed on a screen.
38. **OFW (Overseas Filipino Worker)**: Refers to Filipinos working abroad, contributing significantly to the Philippine economy through remittances.

39. **Balikbayan Box**: A package sent by an OFW to their family in the Philippines, typically filled with gifts, clothing, and other goods.

Conclusion

This glossary provides a foundational understanding of terms and phrases that are integral to navigating life as an expatriate in the Philippines. Familiarity with these words can enhance communication, encourage deeper cultural understanding, and assist in daily activities, legal processes, and social interactions. Expatriates are encouraged to dive deeper into the nuances of the Filipino language and culture to fully start to take in and enrich their experience in the Philippines.

Visit my website at
www.phillipine-investment.com
for more info on investing in the
Philippines!

THANK YOU FOR READING!

MAY WE SEE EACH OTHER IN THE PHILLIPINES!

ISBN: 9798879265705

Made in United States
Troutdale, OR
06/30/2024

20916931R00116